# ASHES
## REGAINED

# Duncan Fletcher

### *with Steve James*

**SIMON &**
**SCHUSTER**

London · New York · Sydney · Toronto

A VIACOM COMPANY

First published in Great Britain by Simon & Schuster UK Ltd in 2005
A Viacom company

1 3 5 7 9 10 8 6 4 2

Simon & Schuster UK Ltd
Africa House
64–78 Kingsway
London WC2B 6AH

Simon & Schuster Australia
Sydney

A CIP catalogue for this book is available
from the British Library.

ISBN: 0-7432-8599-9
EAN: 9780743285995

Typeset in Garamond by M Rules
Printed and bound in Great Britain by
Mackays of Chatham plc

To my incredibly understanding wife, Marina.
If anyone deserves the glory, it is her.

And to our children Nicola and Michael for
their constant love, help and support.

# Acknowledgements

For clarity of reading I have decided to use the surnames of all the England players and management team in this book, but, rest assured, I am much less formal with them when having such fun at cricketing venues around the world and especially in England in the wonderful summer of 2005.

So my thanks and congratulations to the conquering Test squad of Vaughany, Tres, Straussy, Belly, Fred, KP, Jonesy, Gilo, Hoggy, Harmy and Racehorse, and not forgetting Colly. Also to those who played in the one-day series: Goughy, Lewie, Vik, and Kabs; and also Thorpey and Bats who played in the Tests against Bangladesh.

You should be able to work out the surnames of that lot (Racehorse is Simon Jones, in case you're wondering, and Bats is Gareth Batty) but my heartfelt thanks also to my management team, with whom you may be less familiar: to Troy (Cooley, assistant coach), Maaaynaaard (it's a Welsh thing; Matthew Maynard, assistant coach), Stock (Nigel Stockill, physiologist), Phul (I can't pronounce Phil [Neale] properly; operations manager), Kirk (Russell, physio), Wally (Andrew Walpole, media liaison officer), Mark Saxby and Paul Roberts the masseurs, and last but most importantly my mate Deano (Dean Conway, one-day physio).

# ASHES
## REGAINED

# 1

I was quietly confident. I know that it is easy to say that now, but at the start of the summer I did have more than a small inkling that England could win back the Ashes. I said so, too. OK, not in so many words – that would have been reckless, and every pressman in the world knows that I am anything but that in my public pronouncements.

But in an interview at the Vodafone dinner in London prior to the Bangladesh series, Mark Nicholas asked me some searching questions and I decided to put my neck on the block – well, that's how it seemed to me, anyway. I told him I thought that we could have a good summer against the Australians: not exactly stunning headline stuff in itself, but in explaining my reasons I pointed out that we all knew how good the Australians were – they had showed us that in previous years – but could they improve further? I thought that there was only direction in which they could go. In contrast, I said that this summer was going to be very exciting for me, because I did not know how much progress this England side could make. It was my way of saying that I thought there was some vulnerability about the Aussies, and that the Ashes could be ours. Prescient soul, aren't I?

I have long known that the Ashes is the only series by which the English cricketing public – and, of course, the media – will judge the England cricket team. You can do whatever else you like: win other series 3–0, even 4–0; break all manner of records. But it counts for little. Until you have conquered the Australians, then you cannot be considered as the real deal.

That is fair enough, of course. They have been the outstanding side of this generation, and maybe every other one, too. But what irritated me most about the lead-up to the Ashes of 2005 was that there was a reluctance in some quarters to admit that England were making significant progress. When we were hammering the West Indies in 2004 the story was more of their descent than our ascent. New Zealand also came calling last summer and it was billed as a defining series, because they had lost only twice in thirteen Tests. But when we easily disposed of them, there seemed to be more talk of their problems than our advances.

OK, you may be sensing a degree of dissatisfaction here, but in my opinion there was too much negativity out there about English cricket. There was much acclaim, but some of it still seemed begrudging. 'You're beating the rest, but you'll never beat the Aussies,' was the insinuation.

That viewpoint was only reinforced when we defeated South Africa on their own patch in the winter of 2004/05. We did not receive the credit we deserved for that. The South Africans were fortunate that their margin of defeat was only 2–1. It should have been 3–1; that would have been a truer reflection of what happened in that series. Bad light saved them in Durban; we had imploded on day one, but thereafter had dominated. That was our game for the taking. That match was actually a good example of the character of this England side, an illustration of a pattern which has formed over time with this group of players. Quite often they have dug a hole for themselves, but more often than not they have been capable of climbing out of it. That takes character.

Personally I knew how good a side the South Africans were. Yes, they'd had some internal problems, but my knowledge of their domestic cricket told me how many good players they possessed within their system. This was shown in the initial Test squads selected for the International Cricket Council Super Series in Australia, where the South African representation numbered seven (Graeme Smith, Jacques Kallis, Herschelle Gibbs, Mark Boucher, Makhaya Ntini, Shaun Pollock and Andre Nel) compared to only four from England (Michael Vaughan, Andrew Strauss, Andrew Flintoff and Steve Harmison). And, of course, I knew what a proud sporting nation they are. They just do not give up without a fight.

Neither do Australia, but we had not really been in a position to judge that before. My two previous attempts as coach of England against Australia had gone badly. Almost catastrophically, in fact. We lost 4–1 at home in 2001, and by the same margin again, away in the winter of 2002/03. Mind you, I had drawn some strength – if that is the right choice of word – from the fact that we had suffered a debilitating list of injuries in both series. In 2001 Nasser Hussain had missed two Tests, Graham Thorpe four, Vaughan all five, and Ashley Giles four. In 2002/03 the list was even more depressing. Flintoff did not play because of his elongated return from a hernia operation; then Simon Jones suffered his horrible knee injury on the first day at Brisbane. John Crawley bruised a hip and missed the Second and Third Tests; Alec Stewart bruised a hand which ruled him out of the fourth; Andrew Caddick had a sore back which ruled him out of the third; Giles had his wrist broken by Harmison in the nets prior to the second and Harmison himself had sore shins which ruled him out of the first. And that was just those originally selected. The injuries which afflicted the replacements make even harder reading. Chris Silverwood, called up to replace Jones, bowled just four overs before his ankle gave way; Craig White, called up a week into the tour, strained a side and missed the final Test; Alex Tudor, who replaced Darren Gough (whose knee went again), was hit on the head by Brett Lee and the final straw came when Jeremy Snape, who had arrived with the one-day party, had his thumb broken (also by Lee) from the first delivery he faced on tour. That is some list.

I would have liked to have seen what had happened if we had had our full complement throughout those two series. Australia barely had a major concern during those times. What was interesting, though, was that in the final Test of 2002/03 at Sydney, where Australia were without Glenn McGrath and Shane Warne through injury, we beat them soundly. Sadly, that was a dead rubber. But make no mistake: the Australians were trying desperately hard. They wanted a 5–0 whitewash. I would not say that I was now wishing injuries upon Australia because I wanted to beat them at full strength in 2005, but I always wondered what might happen if they suffered injuries to key personnel during the 'live' part of a series; and at the same time we didn't suffer any injuries. We were soon to discover.

But first in 2005 we had to face Bangladesh. There was much talk that it should have been Australia first. 'Catch them cold on damp, seaming pitches,' was the gist of the argument. But I did not go along with that. I wanted the team to have a warm-up series against a lesser side, so that we could regroup and refocus after that series win in South Africa. Admittedly, Bangladesh were not ideal, because they were just too weak. A while ago I might have said that it would have been better to have played Zimbabwe, but sadly they are no better now either. And if you look around the world, all the other Test-playing nations pose a sufficiently difficult challenge. So Bangladesh it was, and we were determined to be ruthless and professional. If we finished them off quickly we could then spend the remaining time practising and training in readiness for Australia.

The build-up, of course, was dominated by a furious debate over the selection of the batting line-up. Mark Butcher had injured a wrist in South Africa, which upon his return home necessitated an operation. At that stage he was still making optimistic noises about being ready for the Ashes, but we knew that we had to plan without him (in the end he did not play for Surrey until August). And number three was a bit of a problem for us. Robert Key had taken over on the South African tour, but had not cemented a place.

After his phenomenal one-day performances in South Africa there was considerable clamour for Kevin Pietersen to be handed a Test place. And I must admit that I was already a big fan. How could I not be after his winter efforts? He was not originally selected for the South African one-day leg of the winter, but he had played just two games in Zimbabwe when I said to Vaughan: 'We've got to get this guy to South Africa.' It was glaringly obvious that he had to be a part of the one-day side which we were attempting to formulate. It was wrongly thought that Pietersen replaced Andrew Flintoff in South Africa. He did not. He was coming anyway. And he made some impression. Three hundreds under the most intense pressure and abuse from his fellow countrymen is not a bad riposte. If you had asked me – off the record, of course! – at the end of that tour whether Pietersen would have started the next Test series, then I would have replied in the affirmative. At that stage I would have considered any re-jigging of the side to accommodate him. But that would have just been me getting carried away by the emotion of the time; not something I am prone to, admittedly.

When it came to the cold light of the English season it was slightly different. I was still keen, but how could the selectors fit him into the Test batting order? There was no way that he could bat at three. He was not even batting at number four for his new county, Hampshire, which worried us a little, especially as inexperienced tyros were being placed above him. He was batting at number five. We had seen how well he could play on the leg-side in the one-day matches, but could he play on the off-side? The thought of Glenn McGrath bowling his relentlessly metronomic off-stump channel made us consider whether Pietersen could cope with that. Had Hampshire seen something we hadn't in placing him so low? Crucially, Pietersen had also made a sluggish start to his Hampshire career, not making the big scores which might have forced our hand. He made a couple of ducks in two of his first four championship innings and did not score his first hundred until the day on which we were meeting to select the squad.

Not that he was the only one struggling in early season. Much had been made of the fact that this was a rare opportunity for the centrally contracted players to spend a longish period with their counties before the Bangladesh series, but the result was some below-par performances. Indeed, the critics quickly pointed out that on the Wednesday before we met to pick the team for the First Test in late May, Strauss became the first contracted batsman to pass a hundred (yes, one hundred) first-class runs for the season – and that it took him seven innings to do so. I thought this might happen. I knew it might be difficult for these players. I liken it to my business background, for, with all due respect, when a centrally contracted England player goes back to county cricket, it is similar to the managing director having to go and work at a lower level in the managerial structure for a week or two. He would doubtless find that much less challenging. That might sound condescending but it is not intended to be. No one can argue that it is not a big step-down in quality, intensity and occasion. I first discovered this when I was coaching at Western

Province between 1993 and 1999. Often I had seven players (Kallis, Gibbs, Gary Kirsten, Brian McMillan, Paul Adams, Craig Matthews and Dave Rundle) – sometimes more – returning from international duty. They always tried their hardest but I could see how difficult it was for them to adjust.

People think that I decry county cricket at every opportunity, but I do not. It should be remembered that I spent two seasons at Glamorgan and enjoyed them thoroughly. There are some very good cricketers in county cricket and some very good cricket played. Is there too much of it? To my mind, yes, but there are plenty of other informed voices within the game who disagree and I do respect their viewpoint.

There was Ian Bell to consider, too. He had made a very promising Test debut against the West Indies at The Oval in 2004, and then showed up well in Zimbabwe and Namibia – albeit against mediocre opposition – in the one-day winter series. The South African one-day leg had not gone quite as smoothly, but he had begun the county championship season with a real bang, including 231 against Middlesex. It was commonly agreed that he had to be the next young batsman in line, having jumped ahead of Key in the queue. However, I was still a little concerned that number three, despite being where Bell batted for Warwickshire, might be a little too high for him at the highest level.

This was when the skipper Vaughan intervened. We had initially dropped him down to number four in the Test batting order because of worries over the effects which the dual load of captaincy and opening might have. That and the eye-catching debut of Strauss at Lord's against the West Indies in 2004, of course. But now Vaughan came to me to say that he wanted to move up to number three. He said that he felt uncomfortable at number four and that, whilst recognising the draining capabilities of captaincy, he considered it to be the right time for elevation. It certainly was; but more than that, this was an encouragingly positive statement of intent from the captain.

Three was sorted then. Who at four and five? Graham Thorpe had done well in South Africa but I was convinced that he could bat no higher than number five. It was a point Nasser Hussain had always been at pains to stress to me, because he felt that Thorpe was too susceptible to the moving ball early in his innings, especially in early season conditions in England. And of course there is no guarantee that those conditions will not persist throughout the summer in England. It can be a hazard all season long, sometimes. Thorpe's increasingly troublesome back problems were not helping, either. And both Vaughan and I were quite adamant that from what we had seen, Pietersen could not bat above number five in Test cricket at that stage of his career. That spot would suit Bell just fine. So it boiled down to Thorpe versus Pietersen for number five.

Thorpe was keen to play – he was on 98 Test caps after all – and Pietersen's lack of runs counted against him. So we decided to go with Thorpe. It was only after we had made this decision that it became known that he had taken up an offer to play and coach in New South Wales in the winter. He came to me while I was having breakfast on the Tuesday morning before the First Test at Lord's. He told me about the job offer and the fact that it was going to go public. He wanted me to know before that happened, which I appreciated. I was very honest with him, though. I said, 'This is going to make things very difficult for me and the other selectors. You are in a unique position.' What I meant was that, of the other England big guns, as I like to term them, who had been nearing retirement during my time as coach, he was the only one who had a young pretender breathing down his neck. That was a young pup barking up the tree by the name of Kevin Pietersen. Mike Atherton and Alec Stewart did not have someone of that calibre pushing them. Neither, at first, did Nasser Hussain. And when he did, with Strauss bursting on to the scene at Lord's with a debut hundred, Hussain immediately called it a day. 'If Pietersen makes lots of runs in the one-day internationals then we are under real pressure,' I told Thorpe, adding that it was now important that he played some cricket and scored a lot of runs.

There was also a worry about Ashley Giles, who had started the county season in fine style with a hatful of wickets for Warwickshire but then picked up a hip cartilage injury while playing against Sussex at Hove. That was a concern because he had become an integral part of our side and we knew that we would struggle to find a viable alternative in the spin department. He was going to be a key player against the Australians, so it was imperative that we got him fit. He was very keen to play but we told him that he could forget about the Tests against Bangladesh; there was no point risking him for that.

There is little point going into too much detail about the two Bangladesh Tests, because, with all due respect, with what was to follow, they have already faded in the memory bank. But what was very important was the meeting we had on the Monday before the First Test. There the team as a whole decided upon its goals for the entire summer. Yes, the Ashes series was already being discussed at this stage, but this was no different from any other summer. When we have two separate Test series we will always set joint goals. Mind you, the goal-setting process was not quite as easy as it had been in the past.

We were to play seven Tests in the summer of 2005. I would hope that we could say that we were confident of winning the two against Bangladesh without sounding arrogant. But for the other five, now that was tricky. It had not been so in the summer of 2004, where I remember that the goal had been an unequiv-ocal 3–0 for the New Zealand series and 4–0 in the following contests against the West Indies. Seven out of seven. And that is what happened. But international cricket is not always as simple as that. Indeed these meetings are rarely simple; they often take a lot of time. In fact when we conducted this same goal-setting meeting in Port Elizabeth before the First Test in South Africa, it took so long that, once the media had discovered that it took place, they were convinced that I had been issuing some stern words to the team in some sort of disciplinary manner. They just would not believe me when I told them that it had simply been a goal-setting meeting.

We always determine our goals by the use of a definitive struc-ture, a series of building blocks divided into three main processes: the WHY, the WHAT and the HOW. The use of this obviously relates back to my days in business, but is nothing more compli-cated than a good example of that old adage: 'If you look after the pennies, the pounds will look after themselves.' That is all we are doing; ensuring that the small things are looked at, so that the bigger things will take care of themselves.

The WHY is the outcome goal which we mentioned above. It was decided by the group that that should be to win five Tests. If you take out the two against Bangladesh, that would mean winning three against Australia. Not a bad call on reflection. If it had not rained at Old Trafford, we would have been correct. But more of that later.

The WHAT are the performance goals in four disciplines: batting, bowling, fielding and the mental aspect of the game. Thus, with the batting, it was our goal to make at least 400 in the first innings of each Test in no more than 130 overs (we did that three times against Australia – they did not do it once). That would entail two hefty partnerships of 200 and 150 from the top order. If things did not go quite according to plan, then we might expect two of 100 and 75 from the lower order. We wanted one batsman to make an individual score of over 150 (Vaughan, at Old Trafford, and Pietersen, at The Oval, managed that).

The bowling goal was simple, as it is for any team: take twenty wickets in the match (three times we did that, even doing so when losing the First Test at Lord's). But it was important that the bowlers thought of restricting the run rate to less than three runs per over; for them to think of bowling maidens. The fielding goal was to take three wickets – targeted as two catches and a run-out. But not any old catches; they would not count. We talk of the type of catches where a bowler knows that it has been the brilliance of the fielder which has captured the wicket. Andrew Strauss's catch at slip to dismiss Adam Gilchrist at Trent Bridge would be an obvious example, although the run-out of Ricky Ponting by substitute Gary Pratt might be considered more obvious given what transpired in its aftermath.

The chat about mental goals would focus upon discipline, enjoyment, body language, energy and support. They are all fairly self-explanatory, and the language of any team-talk in any sport. But they are not blithely bandied about without proper discussion, without reference to specific examples of how we might best use them. The HOW is obviously the actual procedure; the physical actions which need to take place for all of this to come together. We emphasise key words such as concentration, communication and confidence in respect of this, but a common thread is to ensure that we replicate match conditions as closely as we can in practice.

It is important to realise that each individual then has to undergo the same process, using the same structure (the WHY, the WHAT and the HOW) in order to determine their own personal goals. That is entirely self-motivated. Each player is given a sheet on which they lay out their own goals. They then hand that back to me before the first Test of the summer.

That First Test was a rout. As was the Second. We duly won both by an innings and in general they served their purpose, only falling down in as much as they did not provide enough batsmen with practice. Such was the dominance of the top five that no one else got a knock, which did bother me a little. The likes of Flintoff and Geraint Jones could definitely have done with some time in the middle, but we only batted once in each of the matches, so that was that. The matches were Tests, after all, and we always take them seriously, so there was never any thought of messing about by altering batting orders or even changing the side.

Trescothick made two huge centuries, his 194 at Lord's being his first at that ground so that he now has his name up on the honours board. And by following that with 151 in Durham he scooped the man-of-the-series award. But probably the biggest plus was the reappearance of Flintoff from his ankle operation after the Test series in South Africa. He took nine wickets in the two Tests and looked in good fettle since he had only started bowling again a couple of weeks before. Otherwise the bowlers shared the wickets without over-exertion and there seemed to be widespread calls from all quarters for Bangladesh to be stripped of their Test status. That was not for me to worry about. England had won two more Tests and another series, and the Australians were in our sights. That was all that concerned me.

## First Test

*England v. Bangladesh*
*Lord's, London*
*26–28 May 2005*

**Umpires:** K. Hariharan (Ind) and D. Harper (Aus)
**Toss:** England

| Bangladesh: 1st innings | | | R | M | B | 4 | 6 |
|---|---|---|---|---|---|---|---|
| Javed Omar | c Trescothick | b S. Jones | 22 | 81 | 60 | 3 | 0 |
| Nafees Iqbal | c Trescothick | b Harmison | 8 | 40 | 31 | 0 | 0 |
| *Habibul Bashar | c G. Jones | b Hoggard | 3 | 4 | 3 | 0 | 0 |
| Aftab Ahmed | c Strauss | b Flintoff | 20 | 24 | 14 | 5 | 0 |
| Mohammad Ashraful | lbw | b Flintoff | 6 | 14 | 9 | 1 | 0 |
| Mushfiqur Rahim | | b Hoggard | 19 | 85 | 56 | 3 | 0 |
| +Khaled Mashud | lbw | b Hoggard | 6 | 59 | 47 | 0 | 0 |
| Mohammad Rafique | run out (Vaughan/Hoggard) | | 1 | 8 | 3 | 0 | 0 |
| Mashrafe Mortaza | | b Harmison | 0 | 4 | 3 | 0 | 0 |
| Anwar Hossain Monir | not out | | 5 | 13 | 6 | 0 | 0 |
| Shahadat Hossain | c G. Jones | b Hoggard | 4 | 9 | 10 | 1 | 0 |
| Extras | (b 1, lb 1, nb 12) | | 14 | | | | |
| Total | (all out, 38.2 overs, 177 mins) | | 108 | | | | |

FoW: 1–31 (Nafees Iqbal, 9.2 ov), 2–34 (Habibul Bashar, 10.1 ov), 3–65 (Aftab Ahmed, 15.2 ov), 4–65 (Javed Omar, 16.5 ov), 5–71 (Mohammad Ashraful, 17.5 ov), 6–89 (Khaled Mashud, 32.6 ov), 7–94 (Mohammad Rafique, 34.3 ov), 8–98 (Mashrafe Mortaza, 35.3 ov), 9–98 (Mushfiqur Rahim, 36.1 ov), 10–108 (Shahadat Hossain, 38.2 ov).

| Bowling | O | M | R | W |
|---|---|---|---|---|
| Hoggard | 13.2 | 5 | 42 | 4 |
| Harmison | 14 | 3 | 38 | 2 |
| Flintoff | 5 | 0 | 22 | 2 |
| S. Jones | 6 | 4 | 4 | 1 |

| *England: 1st innings* | | | R | M | B | 4 | 6 |
|---|---|---|---|---|---|---|---|
| M. Trescothick | c Mashud | b Rafique | 194 | 367 | 259 | 23 | 0 |
| A. Strauss | lbw | b Mortaza | 69 | 143 | 93 | 10 | 0 |
| *M. Vaughan | c Mashud | b Mortaza | 120 | 203 | 174 | 15 | 0 |
| I. Bell | not out | | 65 | 114 | 94 | 7 | 0 |
| G. Thorpe | not out | | 42 | 95 | 72 | 2 | 0 |
| Extras | (b 4, lb 11, w 3, nb 20) | | 38 | | | | |
| Total | (3 wickets dec, 112 overs, 463 mins) | | 528 | | | | |

DNB: A. Flintoff, +G. Jones, G. Batty, M. Hoggard, S. Harmison, S. Jones.

FoW: 1–148 (Strauss, 29.5 ov), 2–403 (Vaughan, 81.5 ov), 3–415 (Trescothick, 86.1 ov).

| *Bowling* | O | M | R | W |
|---|---|---|---|---|
| Mashrafe Mortaza | 29 | 6 | 107 | 2 |
| Shahadat Hossain | 12 | 0 | 101 | 0 |
| Anwar Hossain Monir | 22 | 0 | 110 | 0 |
| Mohammad Rafique | 41 | 3 | 150 | 1 |
| Aftab Ahmed | 8 | 1 | 45 | 0 |

| Bangladesh: 2nd innings | | | R | M | B | 4 | 6 |
|---|---|---|---|---|---|---|---|
| Javed Omar | c Thorpe | b S. Jones | 25 | 59 | 44 | 3 | 0 |
| Nafees Iqbal | c Flintoff | b Hoggard | 3 | 17 | 11 | 0 | 0 |
| *Habibul Bashar | c Hoggard | b S. Jones | 16 | 31 | 17 | 2 | 0 |
| Aftab Ahmed | lbw | b Hoggard | 32 | 60 | 33 | 6 | 0 |
| Mohammad Ashraful | c Harmison | b Flintoff | 2 | 7 | 7 | 0 | 0 |
| Mushfiqur Rahim | c G. Jones | b Flintoff | 3 | 9 | 9 | 0 | 0 |
| +Khaled Mashud | c Thorpe | b Flintoff | 44 | 117 | 85 | 5 | 0 |
| Mohammad Rafique | c G. Jones | b Harmison | 0 | 2 | 1 | 0 | 0 |
| Mashrafe Mortaza | | b Harmison | 0 | 2 | 1 | 0 | 0 |
| Anwar Hossain Monir | c Trescothick | b S. Jones | 13 | 71 | 42 | 1 | 0 |
| Shahadat Hossain | not out | | 2 | 6 | 3 | 0 | 0 |
| Extras | (b 1, lb 4, nb 14) | | 19 | | | | |
| Total | (all out, 39.5 overs, 195 mins) | | 159 | | | | |

FoW: 1–15 (Nafees Iqbal, 4.1 ov), 2–47 (Habibul Bashar, 10.1 ov), 3–57 (Javed Omar, 12.1 ov), 4–60 (Mohammad Ashraful, 13.3 ov), 5–65 (Mushfiqur Rahim, 15.1 ov), 6–96 (Aftab Ahmed, 22.6 ov), 7–97 (Mohammad Rafique, 23.2 ov), 8–97 (Mashrafe Mortaza, 23.3 ov), 9–155 (Anwar Hossain Monir, 38.3 ov), 10–159 (Khaled Mashud, 39.5 ov).

| Bowling | O | M | R | W |
|---|---|---|---|---|
| Hoggard | 9 | 1 | 42 | 2 |
| Harmison | 10 | 0 | 39 | 2 |
| Flintoff | 9.5 | 0 | 44 | 3 |
| S. Jones | 11 | 3 | 29 | 3 |

**Result:** England won by an innings and 261 runs
**Man of the Match:** M. Trescothick
**Series:** England lead 1–0

## Second Test

*England v. Bangladesh*
*Riverside Ground, Chester-le-Street*
*3–5 June 2005*

**Umpires:** D. Harper (Aus) and A. Hill (NZ)
**Toss:** England

| Bangladesh: 1st innings | | | R | M | B | 4 | 6 |
|---|---|---|---|---|---|---|---|
| Javed Omar | c G. Jones | b Hoggard | 37 | 113 | 83 | 6 | 0 |
| Nafees Iqbal | c Strauss | b Harmison | 7 | 23 | 17 | 0 | 0 |
| *Habibul Bashar | | b Harmison | 6 | 9 | 9 | 1 | 0 |
| Mohammad Ashraful | c G. Jones | b S. Jones | 3 | 13 | 9 | 0 | 0 |
| Rajin Saleh | c Thorpe | b Flintoff | 2 | 28 | 20 | 0 | 0 |
| Aftab Ahmed | c G. Jones | b Harmison | 6 | 53 | 31 | 1 | 0 |
| +Khaled Mashud | c G. Jones | b Harmison | 22 | 64 | 47 | 1 | 0 |
| Mohammad Rafique | c Batty | b Hoggard | 9 | 12 | 9 | 2 | 0 |
| Tapash Baisya | c G. Jones | b Hoggard | 0 | 1 | 2 | 0 | 0 |
| Mashrafe Mortaza | c G. Jones | b Harmison | 1 | 11 | 5 | 0 | 0 |
| Anwar Hossain Monir | | not out | 0 | 20 | 11 | 0 | 0 |
| Extras | (lb 2, w 5, nb 4) | | 11 | | | | |
| Total | (all out, 39.5 overs, 178 mins) | | 104 | | | | |

FoW: 1–17 (Nafees Iqbal, 5.5 ov), 2–27 (Habibul Bashar, 7.5 ov), 3–34 (Mohammad Ashraful, 10.6 ov), 4–42 (Rajin Saleh, 17.3 ov), 5–59 (Javed Omar, 26.1 ov), 6–69 (Aftab Ahmed, 29.6 ov), 7–87 (Mohammad Rafique, 32.3 ov), 8–87 (Tapash Baisya, 32.5 ov), 9–93 (Mashrafe Mortaza, 35.1 ov), 10–104 (Khaled Mashud, 39.5 ov).

| Bowling | O | M | R | W |
|---|---|---|---|---|
| Hoggard | 12 | 6 | 24 | 3 |
| Harmison | 12.5 | 2 | 38 | 5 |
| S. Jones | 8 | 2 | 26 | 1 |
| Flintoff | 7 | 3 | 14 | 1 |

| England: 1st innings | | | R | M | B | 4 | 6 |
|---|---|---|---|---|---|---|---|
| M. Trescothick | c Ashraful | b Ahmed | 151 | 192 | 148 | 21 | 2 |
| A. Strauss | lbw | b Mortaza | 8 | 34 | 30 | 1 | 0 |
| *M. Vaughan | c Mashud | b Mortaza | 44 | 53 | 40 | 9 | 0 |
| I. Bell | not out | | 162 | 233 | 168 | 25 | 1 |
| G. Thorpe | not out | | 66 | 129 | 85 | 7 | 0 |
| Extras | (b 1, lb 10, w 2, nb 3) | | 16 | | | | |
| Total | (3 wickets dec, 78 overs, 322 mins) | | 447 | | | | |

DNB: A. Flintoff, +G. Jones, G. Batty, M. Hoggard, S. Harmison, S. Jones.

FoW: 1–18 (Strauss, 8.1 ov), 2–105 (Vaughan, 20.4 ov), 3–260 (Trescothick, 45.5 ov).

| Bowling | O | M | R | W |
|---|---|---|---|---|
| Mashrafe Mortaza | 22 | 4 | 91 | 2 |
| Tapash Baisya | 15 | 2 | 80 | 0 |
| Mohammad Rafique | 18 | 0 | 107 | 0 |
| Anwar Hossain Monir | 15 | 1 | 102 | 0 |
| Aftab Ahmed | 8 | 0 | 56 | 1 |

| Bangladesh: 2nd innings | | | R | M | B | 4 | 6 |
|---|---|---|---|---|---|---|---|
| Javed Omar | c G. Jones | b Harmison | 71 | 131 | 108 | 11 | 0 |
| Nafees Iqbal | c G. Jones | b Flintoff | 15 | 46 | 29 | 2 | 0 |
| Rajin Saleh | c Strauss | b Flintoff | 7 | 34 | 30 | 1 | 0 |
| Mohammad Ashraful | c Hoggard | b Batty | 12 | 32 | 31 | 1 | 0 |
| *Habibul Bashar | lbw | b Flintoff | 63 | 75 | 52 | 11 | 0 |
| +Khaled Mashud | lbw | b Hoggard | 25 | 99 | 79 | 3 | 0 |
| Aftab Ahmed | not out | | 82 | 102 | 82 | 13 | 1 |
| Mohammad Rafique | | b Hoggard | 2 | 6 | 3 | 0 | 0 |
| Anwar Hossain Monir | c Thorpe | b Hoggard | 0 | 9 | 5 | 0 | 0 |
| Tapash Baisya | c G. Jones | b Hoggard | 18 | 40 | 26 | 2 | 0 |
| Mashrafe Mortaza | c Trescothick | b Hoggard | 0 | 3 | 3 | 0 | 0 |
| Extras | (lb 6, w 1, nb 14) | | 21 | | | | |
| Total | (all out, 72.5 overs, 293 mins) | | 316 | | | | |

FoW: 1–50 (Nafees Iqbal, 11.3 ov), 2–75 (Rajin Saleh, 20.3 ov), 3–101 (Mohammad Ashraful, 29.5 ov), 4–125 (Javed Omar, 34.3 ov), 5–195 (Habibul Bashar, 49.1 ov), 6–235 (Khaled Mashud, 58.5 ov), 7–245 (Mohammad Rafique, 60.2 ov), 8–251 (Anwar Hossain Monir, 62.1 ov), 9–311 (Tapash Baisya, 72.1 ov), 10–316 (Mashrafe Mortaza, 72.5 ov).

| Bowling | O | M | R | W |
|---|---|---|---|---|
| Hoggard | 15.5 | 3 | 73 | 5 |
| Harmison | 17 | 1 | 86 | 1 |
| S. Jones | 10 | 1 | 49 | 0 |
| Flintoff | 15 | 2 | 58 | 3 |
| Batty | 15 | 2 | 44 | 1 |

**Result:** England won by an innings and 27 runs
**Man of the Match:** M. Hoggard
**Series:** England won 2–0
**Players of the Series:** M. Trescothick (Eng) and Javed Omar (Bang)

# 2

In September 2004, England had beaten Australia by six wickets in the semi-final of the ICC Champions Trophy at Edgbaston. Even though we went on to lose the final in agonising fashion against the West Indies, we never forgot about that victory in the build-up to the Ashes summer of 2005. Many had said that it was a one-off success, into which little should be read. But we knew differently. It was a clinical performance and some hugely important psychological hurdles had been overcome. It was time to feed off them in the run-up to the multitude of one-day matches which were to precede the Ashes. These, which were to include the triangular NatWest Series and the NatWest Challenge (three matches against Australia), began with a Twenty20 clash against the Australians at Southampton's Rose Bowl in June.

It had been suggested that England pick a side especially for that match, comprising county stalwarts with experience of the shortest format of the game. Names like Leicestershire's Darren Maddy were bandied around as being those whom we should look at. It was argued that not many of the England team had significant experience of Twenty20 – Michael Vaughan had never played a game of it, for instance. Even my knowledge of the format was brought into question. But I was adamant that we had to pick the same group of players which we were intending to use for those later games. What experience did the Australians have of it anyway? And if we did happen to beat them with a specially tailored team – which I thought unlikely, because I always feel that your best cricketers are your best cricketers, full stop – what confidence could then be taken into the rest of the matches? Absolutely none.

We wanted to use the Twenty20 match as practice, but also as a statement of intent. We had a little more know-how of Twenty20 than the Aussies, especially with Matthew Maynard having joined us as assistant coach – he had been one of the leading English-qualified batsmen in the competition in 2004. He had now been confirmed in a permanent position with the ECB. He had done well during the winter in southern Africa and it was originally planned that he would just be with us for the one-day segment of the summer, while continuing to play for Glamorgan for the rest of the summer. However, an odd sequence of events dictated otherwise. He played just one championship match before being struck down by pneumonia, during which it dawned on him that he no longer had the appetite or desire to play full-time. The coaching had enthused him during the winter, and that was what he now wanted to do. I was very happy with that, because I had long wanted to include him in my set-up; ever since we had met at Glamorgan in 1997, when he was captain, and I realised what a fertile cricketing brain he had. In fact I had considered doing so two years previously, but decided against it because I did not want to deprive Glamorgan of their best batsman. I felt guilty enough about what had happened in 1999 when I left the Welsh county for England, just one season into a three-year contract. I had also taken Glamorgan physio Dean Conway with me, too.

Loyalty has always been a fundamental quality in my life – ever since my schooldays at Prince Edward in Harare (or Salisbury, as it was then), where it was drummed into us – and I still feel a little uneasy about the manner in which my time at Glamorgan ended. Not that there was any ill-feeling on their part – far from it – but it was unsatisfactory from my point of view. With the benefit of hindsight I might have been better off leaving Glamorgan halfway through the season, once it was announced that I was to take the England job. Glamorgan were struggling, and all the while England were being humbled by New Zealand. I was caught in the middle.

But now with Maynard to look after the batting and Troy Cooley the bowling – a superb coach, with whom I hit it off immediately – I had my ideal back-up coaching team. When we met as a team before that Twenty20 – in the little time we had after the Bangladesh Tests – it was decided that we had to be aggressive towards the Australians straight away. That meant 'getting into their space', as I always like to say to the players – although not as much as 'coming to the party', and all those other sayings which the press seem to delight in picking up on as my staple fare. But it is still a recurring phrase. And it was probably more so this summer than at any other time – inside the dressing room, at least. And in general, the players responded.

We really wanted to show some overt aggression in this match, which would surprise not only the Australians but a whole host of other observers, because bowling in Twenty20 is normally considered a damage-limitation exercise. 'Leave your ego in the dressing room,' Mike Kasprowicz once said during his time at Glamorgan, but that was not our thinking. In fact it was the complete opposite. We wanted to bowl a lot of short balls, and there were certain batsmen whom we identified as special targets for that tactic. Andrew Symonds was one, and the first ball he received from Darren Gough – a bristling bouncer even though he was on a hat-trick, followed by an angry glare – epitomised the attitude we wanted to exude in this match. Gough had been on fire in the warm-up match beforehand against Hampshire, where he had taken a hat-trick in a one-sided match, which we won by 153 runs. It was over so quickly that we played a 12 overs per side match afterwards. That naturally attracted some criticism but I thought it was a powerful statement of our desire to play; to achieve the required amount of practice. Our bowling and batting under pressure had obviously not been tested in that first game.

Gough rolled back the years in that Twenty20 with some real aggression in a wonderful bowling performance (3–16 from his three overs), which saw the Australians dismissed for just 79, losing seven wickets for just eight runs in 3.2 overs. And Gloucestershire's Jon Lewis, whom we had had an eye on for a while, took four wickets on his international debut, after we had posted an excellent score of 179 due to useful contributions from Marcus Trescothick, Kevin Pietersen and Paul Collingwood. In terms of our batting we had talked about just thinking of it as a shortened version of a fifty-over game. That might sound obvious and simplistic, but what it meant was that the batsmen did not panic; keeping wickets in hand was vital, as was giving a batsman time to 'get himself in'. It was not to be a case of everyone trying to hit his first ball out of the park. It seemed to work.

One should never underestimate the value of that win. It was as clinical as that ICC Champions Trophy success of 2004. The enthusiasm and intensity were magnificent, setting the tone for the rest of the summer. It also produced the first rendition of our new team song. It is something I have long wanted, and I mentioned this to Maynard in Namibia during the winter. 'Leave it to me,' he said typically. He had been captain of Glamorgan in 2000 when they had introduced a team song, so he did have some experience of this sort of thing. Or at least he knew a man who did. He spoke to Owen Parkin, the former Glamorgan bowler, who had composed the lyrics for their song, and, sure enough, by the time of this match everything was in place. We had copies of the lyrics printed for everyone to sing from at first (unfortunately some were still using them at the end of the summer!) and we gave it our best singing voice. It has caught on and is now sung with real fervour, with the whole squad and management in a huddle every time that we win. Only when we win, though, do we sing it. It became louder as the summer went on.

It was also sweet to dent the Australians' pride at Southampton. They had arrived amid supercilious predictions that they might be able to emulate the 'Invincibles' of 1948. Well, after this most comprehensive performance, we were reminding ourselves that we had now beaten them twice on the trot. There might also just have been the odd chuckle around the camp when the score from Taunton was heard later two days later: Somerset had managed to chase down 343 to win in another one-day match.

In the aftermath of the Twenty20 victory, which seemed to grip the nation not only with its efficiency, but also its atmosphere and excitement, there was obviously considerable clamour for there to be more international matches of that duration. Funnily enough, those calls seemed to have died down by the end of the summer, given the exhilarating manner of almost everything that followed. But what I did say at the time was that although I thought that there was a role for international Twenty20, the schedulers needed to be careful, because it could only be fitted in if the number of matches in one of the other formats was reduced. That is where people always used to get confused when I called for England to play more one-day internationals. They can only do that if they play fewer Tests. And that was what I was advocating too. People were saying, 'He wants more one-day internationals and he wants more rest at the same time – what is he on about?' Fewer Tests, that's what. For those involved, the amount of international cricket currently being played is already mountainous, although I am also mindful of the huge appetite in this country for the game at this level.

One only has to look at what happened this summer to realise that.

So we began our NatWest Series by entertaining Bangladesh at The Oval. Any concerns over complacency were dispelled by an emphatic ten-wicket victory, with Trescothick (100 not out) and Andrew Strauss (82 not out) easily knocking off the runs. For Trescothick it was a special day; a third successive hundred (to add to the two Test efforts) on his 100th one-day international appearance. Those three knocks might have only been against Bangladesh but they were important because, like everyone else, he had struggled a little in early season.

The bigger talking-point, though, was the fact that Strauss had opened; he had been batting at number four in one-day cricket for some time, with Geraint Jones opening. That was a strategy we had persevered with for a while, to the obvious chagrin of some observers. We had experimented with Jones at number three in the summer of 2004 but then in South Africa had decided to let him open. It was felt – and not just by me (by Michael Vaughan and many other senior players too) – that his attacking style was best suited to that role, especially to take advantage of the fielding restrictions in the first fifteen overs. We also felt that he had the technique to go on and make substantial scores. In contrast, we thought that Strauss was better suited to the middle overs where he could knock the ball around from number four, utilising his strengths square of the wicket. Four is the pivotal position in the batting order for me in one-day cricket. The player fulfilling that role has to be very mentally strong and adaptable too. He might have to see the innings through if there have been early wickets, or he might have to realise that he could be dropped down the order should there be a flying start, thus necessitating an earlier introduction of the big-hitters.

For one reason or another the Jones experiment did not work out. He was not helped in South Africa by the fact that none of the others in the top three were making runs; there were only two fifties from them in seven matches. The strategy was correct in my opinion, and it was not as if he was being dismissed for exceptionally low scores every time. Often he was getting 'in' and then getting out. The problem can only have been a mental one. If we made a mistake, it was in not realising that in South Africa Jones had been the only player to have featured in every single match of that tour, stretching right back to the one-dayers in Namibia. And remembering how arduous a task wicketkeeping is, that was an oversight. Most of the players were tired, naturally so after such a long tour, but he must have been the most fatigued of them all. But I do think that if we had been playing in the sub-continent (and he was not so tired!) he would have succeeded in his role. But he struggled on some seaming pitches and it was best to change tack, because mentally it might have been of long-term detriment. I'm sure that it will be revisited, though.

Off we went to Bristol to face Australia, where another surprise lay in store. As we prepared on the Saturday, Australia were playing Bangladesh in Cardiff. We had delighted in the Australians' discomfort that week, but it had never crossed our minds that they might lose that match. So there we were in Bristol having a team management meeting when news filtered through that the Bangladeshis had won. I can only describe that revelation as incredible. What is more, Andrew Symonds had enjoyed the renowned hospitality of the Cardiffians a little too eagerly and been dropped for his inappropriate behaviour. It all added up to severe embarrassment for the Australians, and could only hand us a huge psychological advantage. The next day, that showed. Indeed, it heralded a new experience for me as coach against Australia. In the past I would have been walking on to the field on the morning of the game, asking myself: 'How are we going to win this game? What are we going to have to do right to win this game?' Now, I walked on with a spring in my step, thinking: 'It will be really nice to beat them again today.' That's how confident I was that day. There was a positive buzz about the camp that meant I knew that we could win again. And it was not just because the Australians added to their week of travails by being caught up in traffic and being late out on to the ground for pre-match practice.

However, it was not all plain sailing. We bowled superbly to restrict them to 252–9 on a good pitch with short boundaries. Steve Harmison took 5–33 and thoroughly deserved such flattering figures – his best in one-day cricket. In fact, in terms of line and length I am not sure that I have seen him bowl better in any form of cricket. It was obvious that the Australians did not enjoy facing him, with the tactic of liberal short-pitched balls to the fore. And he was helped by a stupendous catch from Collingwood at backward point to dismiss Matthew Hayden. It was one of the greatest I've ever seen, even better than

Collingwood's effort the previous year at Headingley to get rid of Ramnaresh Sarwan. It is no fluke that he is able to take such breathtaking catches. We spend hours working together to perfect things like that. We practise realistically with him standing in that backward point position and someone throwing the ball to me to carve it in that direction. We also do something similar with Ashley Giles so that he can replicate fielding in the gully.

We then got ourselves into trouble with the bat, falling behind the rate to 160–6 before we were rescued by Kevin Pietersen, whose 91 not out was truly a match-winning knock. His previous hundreds in South Africa had all been in a losing cause but this was different; he was so cool under the pressure. He's just such a positive individual, who thrives on the challenges posed by the international game. The Aussies could throw whatever they liked at him, but he would just stand there and prove himself with his batting. And that is what he did here. I appreciated the way he read the situation; he was so streetwise in his approach. He began cautiously, had a look at the pitch, assessed what he needed to do, and then bang! Some of the Australian bowlers, Jason Gillespie in particular, did not seem to know what had hit them. Credit must also go to Lewis, who came in at the end and played very calmly on his home ground. But Pietersen was the hero. And I could see a headache looming – not from any celebrations! – but from the selection dilemma which was now re-presenting itself. The clamour for Pietersen to play in the forthcoming Tests was re-emerging, and rightly so. And meanwhile Graham Thorpe was barely playing at all because of his back injury. Were we to go for Pietersen's positive brand of batting, which took the attack to Australia, or Thorpe, whose forte was crisis-management, in itself a negative mindset because it presumed that we would already be in trouble for him to thrive?

I was annoyed, though, that yet again we had let a bowler like Brad Hogg cause us so much trouble with his left-arm wrist spin. By whichever means we had been unable to manoeuvre him around, and he is no Shane Warne or Muttiah Muralitharan; no world-class spinner for whom you have to adopt special tactics.

Playing spin is obviously an issue which is close to my heart, and one which has caused a good deal of controversy within media circles. That is because of my preference for the sweep and slog/sweep shots. They were shots I used a lot during my time playing for Zimbabwe and I have always been convinced that they have to be a part of the armoury of any top batsman. Especially if he is to succeed in the sub-continent against the top-quality spin you encounter there on slow, turning pitches. The problem is that a lot of the commentators in this country do not concur. Some of them have been conducting a long-running campaign against England batsmen sweeping. They argue that the best way to do that is to hit them over the top, using a straight bat rather than the horizontal blade of the sweep or slog/sweep.

I do not actually advise against hitting over the top – in fact I actively encourage it once a batsman has settled against a spinner, or when he is batting on a good pitch which is not turning. But my first option would always be the sweep. For evidence, consider this comparison: when you are playing a spinner, there are three things you have to determine as a batsman. First, how much is the ball going to spin? That can be taken out of the equation by the sweep because you can smother it. If you are coming down the pitch to hit over the top you don't know how much it is going to turn, which can lead to problems, especially as you are not looking to get to the pitch of the ball (you cannot get the required elevation if you do that). Second, how much is the ball going to bounce? That can again be dealt with by the sweep, but not so by the hit over the top – thus why should you sweep on unpredictable pitches, and hit over the top on more predictable ones? And third, how fast is the ball travelling? That judgement has to be made whichever shot you play. The sweep has negated two out of three judgements. It looks like the better option to me.

One of the major objectives of the sweep shot is to force the spinner and his captain to position a fielder on the 45 (degrees) – a short fine leg, in other words. By manipulating the field in that way it will open up gaps in front of the bat.

I must emphasise that I do not advocate that batsmen concentrate on the sweep and slog/sweep to the exclusion of all other shots. Decisions still have to be made by the batsmen, but options have to be made available to him and he must appreciate them. Where they are crucial is on slow, unpredictable, turning pitches where they are the best option.

Support for this preference came in an article by Derek Pringle in the *Daily Telegraph* during the summer about playing spin: 'Before the 1987 World Cup semi-final between England and India in Bombay,' Pringle wrote, 'Graham Gooch took one look at the dry, dusty pitch prepared for India's spinners and decided the sweep was the only shot that was going to bring runs. Instead of batting in the nets against England's bowlers, Gooch summoned the locals to bowl at him. For the next thirty minutes he attempted to sweep every ball regardless of length or line. While team-mates looked on perplexed, all became clear a day later when England won with 115 runs from Gooch, most of them swept.

'Matthew Hayden worked on something similar on Australia's 2000/01 tour of India. Although he had a reputation for bullying bowlers, he was considered vulnerable against spin. Like Gooch he practised sweep after sweep, including the slog sweep, which during matches often sailed into the stands for six.'

Despite what they often say, most spinners do not enjoy being swept, because it disrupts their sense of which length to bowl. Sometimes you hear them saying, 'I love it when a batsman sweeps me.' That is just reverse psychology in my book. Muralitharan is one who often says that, but I have watched him closely when he has been swept early on in his spell. His walk back to his mark has always been a very timid one in that instance; the walk of a man who does not like what he is seeing.

Anyway, none of this was particularly relevant in our next game, against Bangladesh at Trent Bridge, where a glut of records were toppled. As a team, that is a subject we have often addressed. We want to make history. It goes without saying that in order to do that we have to perform some amazing feats. It might only have been against Bangladesh again, but that is exactly what we did in Nottingham, as we won by 168 runs. For a start Collingwood became the first man to score a century and take six wickets in a one-day international. He hit 112 not out, sharing a stand of 210 with Strauss as we reached a national record of 391–4 in the day–night match. Strauss's 152 was the third-highest score by an England batsman in one-day internationals, behind only Robin Smith's 167 not out against Australia in 1993 and David Gower's 158 versus New Zealand in 1982/83. And Collingwood's was the second-fastest ever by an England batsman, requiring only eight more balls than Pietersen's 69-ball effort against South Africa in East London on the tour there last winter. Collingwood's 6–31 then just happened to be England's best-ever one-day bowling figures. Not a bad night for him, then.

And naturally I was delighted. He has always been a cricketer with whom I have enjoyed working: he works hard in practice, but it is his on-field attitude which I like most. He is not afraid of anything or anyone, and, as any all-rounder should be, is always doing something in the game. I think that it is unfair that he has been all too readily tagged with the classification of a 'bits and pieces cricketer'. He is better than that. When people question me about that, I always ask them, 'What were players like Australia's Ian Harvey or Andrew Symonds like when they first came into international cricket?' I bet that if they had been English, then they would have been saddled with a similar reputation to Collingwood. It is one of the most common faults among critics and pundits that they do not remember what the best international cricketers were like when they first started in international cricket. A very good international cricketer will leave the scene and then the poor youngster selected to take his place is compared to the retiree when he was at the peak of his powers, rather than when he began his career, just like the youngster now is.

Collingwood has the ability to become a top-quality all-rounder at international level, certainly in the one-day game at least. He does have to develop his bowling a bit further, but he is continually working on that, especially on using different variations. They proved useful on this slow Trent Bridge pitch.

It was also good to see Hampshire's Chris Tremlett take four wickets on his debut. He might have got a hat-trick too, but when Mohammad Ashraful defended his first ball into the ground it bounced on to the top of the stumps without dislodging the bails. Tremlett was someone we had been tracking for a while and it was good to have a look at him in circumstances which could be described as relatively relaxing for an international match, especially against opponents whom we knew would struggle with the bounce which his 6 foot 7 inch frame naturally creates. That also caused our batsmen quite a few problems in the nets throughout the summer; many of them said that they found Tremlett just as difficult as facing Harmison, maybe even more testing. We shall come later to some convincing evidence of that before the Second Test at Edgbaston.

The only downside of that Nottingham victory was a slight groin strain picked up by skipper Vaughan. With a match against Australia in Durham only two days later he was always going to be struggling. 'Here we go again – injuries before an Ashes series,' I thought to myself. It meant that Trescothick took over as captain and had a very important decision to make upon winning the toss in this day–night match. He decided to bowl. I say 'he' but it was a collective decision, of which I was very much a part. With the benefit of hindsight it might look a poor decision because Australia made 266–5 and we lost by 57 runs, but it was made after much consideration. And not only that, there was investigation too. We were keen to field first for a couple of reasons. First, we considered ourselves a good chasing side, having already done that twice successfully in the series. Second, we thought that the confidence of the Australian batsmen was such that they were struggling to set targets; that they were unsure of what a good total was on the varying pitches and grounds on which they were playing.

We had two Durham players with us in Harmison and Collingwood, and they confirmed to us that the lights at Chester-le-Street generally did not have that much effect. It was thought that the pitch might provide some assistance to the seam bowlers and then improve as the game wore on. Unfortunately that did not prove to be the case as a sluggish pitch deteriorated. We lost early wickets and that was that. Darren Gough with 46 not out was our highest scorer – that says it all.

But we qualified for the final by easily beating Bangladesh at Headingley. That was a novel experience in my tenure as coach, because normally we were sweating until the last game to be sure of progressing to the final. It demonstrated clearly that we were making progress as a one-day unit. It would be easy to be critical and say that the third side were only Bangladesh, but it must be remembered that we had beaten Australia at Bristol. Even if there is a perceived weak link, you do not qualify early unless you defeat the other fancied side at least once. Here at Leeds Flintoff bowled magnificently, taking 4–9, and Strauss demonstrated his continuing adaptation to the one-day opener's role with a well-made 98, just missing out on a hundred when having a bit of a slog at the end.

No matter. The summer was about to really hot up. Ask anyone now for their most vivid recollection of this NatWest series and it will probably be a steamy afternoon at Edgbaston, where this England side showed that they were really going to stand up to Australia. The image will be of Matthew Hayden standing toe-to-toe with bowler Simon Jones. Hayden had hit the ball back to Jones, who in a completely reactionary piece of cricket, had thrown it back. He was obviously aiming at the stumps, and had no intention of hitting Hayden. However, he did miss by a fair distance, and the ball hit Hayden in the chest. Hayden went apoplectic, walking menacingly down the pitch and screaming at Jones.

What happened next really pleased me. Jones was not left on his own as he went down the pitch to apologise; not isolated like some England players might have been in the past. I thought that Jones's body language was good; it was obvious that he wanted to apologise but he was also saying, 'You're not intimidating me.' His team-mates rushed to his aid. We had talked about this – not about conducting mass verbal jousts, of course, but about putting the Australians in their place if they came at us aggressively. That is what Hayden did. He was the one trying to intimidate. Collingwood rushed in, as did Strauss and Vaughan. I thought they did it in a classy way – if classy is the right word. If I am honest, I am not sure which adjective to use, but what I am trying to say is that there are ways and means of sorting out incidents on a cricket field. Because they do happen: they always will in the heat of battle. And I thought we did it 'in the right manner' there.

It was not roughhouse behaviour; rather, they told Hayden exactly what they thought and that was it. And it should be remembered that Hayden was out lbw – to a beautiful Jones in-swinger – not long after. It was also a shame that it rained: I fancied us to win that game.

I thought the incident showed magnificent team spirit. I also think that it was a seminal moment in the summer that was unfolding. It shook the Australians. There had been a psychological shift in pressure and pride. They now knew they were in for a battle, and we began to see flaws in their behaviour. For it was here that it was alleged that Hayden had sworn at a child as he came out to bat. I know that the Australians were not happy about having to run through the guard of honour made at these games by young children waving flags of St George. We had become aware of it at Durham, where it appeared that one of the Australian players had ripped a flag from the hands of one of the children.

If the Australians were unhappy with having to endure some patriotism, this was nothing. What about the nationalistic behaviour we have to deal with when we go to Australia? It is much worse than any of this. The last time we were there, we were invited to a dinner in Perth as guests of honour. There a comedian humiliated us. We just had to sit there and take it. At one stage Alec Stewart was about to get up and leave. By contrast, what the Australians were now experiencing were minor issues. But the good news from England's point of view was that they seemed to be allowing themselves to be distracted by them. They were rattled.

That might have been why they had another slight stutter against Bangladesh in Canterbury. They certainly did not have things all their own way again, with the Bangladeshis scoring 250–8, and Australia were 83–3 at one stage before easing home by six wickets.

And that brought us to the final at Lord's, which ended in a tie, of all things. Overall I was disappointed because I thought that we should have won after bowling them out for 196. Not that I thought that it would be a stroll in the park either; watching someone like Symonds play out three maidens suggested that there was something in the pitch for the bowlers. But we had bowled well, especially Harmison and Flintoff, who took three wickets apiece. I was also pleased with the manner in which we fought back after being in the mire at 33–5 in our innings. Geraint Jones and Collingwood came together and played superbly in putting on 116. I have already mentioned Collingwood's character, but Jones is hewn from similar stone. That is why I have always been keen to play the pair of them and they vindicated my faith here. Jones, especially, was copping some flak at the time – as he often does – but he also took five catches and scooped the man-of-the-match award. He is a quality batsman/wicketkeeper, who fits the bill we are looking for – a batsman who can keep wicket. I am a great believer that you can teach someone to catch the ball, but you cannot teach someone to bat or hit the ball effectively. Jones makes some mistakes behind the stumps, but so do other wicketkeepers around the world, without the attendant fuss and outcry. Jones can bat, of that you can be sure.

Mind you, having done all that hard work, one of either Jones or Collingwood should have gone on to complete the job, but as so often happens, once one of them went, so did the other. So it was left to Giles and Gough to inch us close. It came down to our needing three off the last ball, with Giles facing Glenn McGrath. There was an enormous appeal for lbw and, amid the confusion, the pair managed to scramble two runs for a tie. They were given as runs anyway, but I don't think that the ball did manage to shave Giles's inside edge. Not that I thought the appeal was out either; I thought that Giles was outside the line of off-stump.

It's funny because I do not think that leg-byes should be allowed in cricket; you are basically rewarding the batsman for having failed in his mission, which is to hit the ball. And I know that there are a lot of other people who agree with that, but I also know how difficult it is for things to be changed. And I'm not sure that I would have been moaning about leg-byes if they had been given instead of runs off the last ball in this game!

The way I think about cricket, and all other sports for that matter, is quite lateral. To take the game forward one must conjure up new ideas and innovations which might be introduced. My well-documented suggestion that both the fielding and batting sides should be able to refer three of the umpires' decisions in each innings to the TV third umpire is an example. I am not sure that anyone truly understands this system. I have tried on numerous occasions to explain it, but there seems to have been something lost in the translation along the way.

I will explain again briefly. Each side has three referrals in each innings of a match. So let us say that a batsman edges the ball behind. The fielders then appeal. What is crucial is that the umpire makes a decision immediately. That is essential because you still need to be able to judge whether he is a good umpire or not, and probably more importantly, you need to remember that at lower levels there will be no television replays. If the umpire then says not out, the fielding side can appeal, but they only have ten seconds in which to decide to make that referral. They must make it as quickly as the umpire has to make his decision, otherwise you would have long conferences and the game would be slowed down considerably. If the third umpire then says that the batsman did edge the ball, he is given out and the fielding side keep their three referrals. On the other hand if the third umpire ruled that the batsman was not out, then the fielding side would be reduced to two referrals.

Also if the batsman was given out and he thought that he did not edge it, then he could refer – in ten seconds, of course. If the third umpire rules not out, the batsman stays and his side keeps three referrals. If he is ruled out, then they are down to two.

It might sound rather complicated, but I do not think that it is. If the technology cannot make a definitive decision, then the on-field umpire's original decision stands (and the three referrals still stand). It would not take long for the players to become accustomed to it. And I think that it would help the umpires because the players would be part of their process. The umpires have a hugely difficult task and have my sympathy. I have done some umpiring myself – not at first-class level, granted, but at league standard – and I know what it is like. What I also know is that if an umpire walks away and knows that he has made a mistake, it will affect him in some way for the rest of the day. That is only human nature.

With this system, if the umpires did make a mistake, then it could be corrected, and they could be more relaxed for the rest of the day. There would be less appealing and sides would only refer if they were certain that they would 'win'. They would not want to be wasting referrals early on, especially if a close finish was in prospect. It could also expose the more selfish batsmen. If they unnecessarily use up a referral by taking a chance, just imagine the reaction in the dressing room. At least it might mean that the players are engaging in a furious debate among themselves rather than directing their anger at the poor umpire out in the middle, as is usually the case.

There is the entertainment aspect to be considered as well. This is probably the most important factor. At the moment, contentious decisions are not shown on the big screens at grounds. With this system they could be. No replays would be shown (not even in the dressing room or to the third umpire) until the time has elapsed for the referral to be called – otherwise you can imagine crafty coaches signalling from the balcony – but once it is called, then spectators could feel that they were part of the process as the replays are shown on the big screen. They would love it. Just think of the excitement already generated at home – and in dressing rooms too – when there is a close decision being replayed. Everybody wants to be the umpire in those scenarios. Now they really could be.

I thought that all this was a good idea. But the ICC has deemed otherwise. They think that such system would be flying in the face of one of the fundamental maxims of the game, namely that the umpire's decision is final. I think my system would be helping the umpires. It won't stop me or others thinking of other ways to innovate, though.

I am intrigued by the fact that the ICC decided to bring in the use of technology for all decisions in the Super Series in Australia. I thought that they might have learned lessons from their Champions Trophy in Sri Lanka in 2002, where the umpires were also able to refer any decision to the third umpire. It resulted in the umpires not wanting to make any decisions – and who could blame them? – because they had the technology to refer to. There was confusion too, because the third umpire was not permitted to offer any additional information to that which was requested by the on-field umpire. Thus I remember a game in that tournament in which England were involved where the umpire on the field was heard to ask the third umpire of a fielder: 'Did he take that catch cleanly?'

'Yes, he did,' replied the man looking at the television screen, 'but the batsman did not nick it.'

'I just asked you whether he caught it,' said the on-field official, and the batsman was given out. Erroneously.

Anyway, back to this NatWest series. I thought that we had come of age as a one-day team here. In this form of the game we had previously been horribly inconsistent during my tenure as England coach, but now I could see that it was possible for us to make the same progressions as we had in the Test arena. We were as good as, if not better, than Australia in this one-day series. And again I'm not sure if they were happy to come to terms with that reality. That manifested itself in the so-called 'war of words' between myself and John Buchanan afterwards.

As you might have noticed, I am naturally reticent and guarded when it comes to press conferences, but there are odd occasions when public utterances can work for, as opposed to against, you. So when I was asked by an Australian journalist after the final whether I thought that psychologically we had won the final, I replied that, yes, I thought we had. I probably should not have added that there were certain aspects of the match that showed that. As soon as I said that, I knew that I would have to explain myself, and sure enough, the question came rebounding back.

'What are they then?' asked the journalist.

To me, my reply was pretty harmless but, boy, was a big deal later made of it. I was actually trying to praise the England team for winning quite a few mini-battles in the final, rather than attempting to denigrate the Australians. I said that there were three things which had struck me as demonstrating that this was an Australian side under pressure; a team acting very differently from their previous omnipotence.

The first factor I remarked upon was that I had never seen an

Australian side being captained by committee before. In the final match, there was the rather strange sight of Ricky Ponting being surrounded by three or four other players who were all lending the skipper the benefit of their advice. I enjoyed seeing that, even though I do not think that I was necessarily pointing the finger at Ponting with that observation. The second factor was that never before had I seen an Australian batsman being protected, as McGrath was at the end of their innings by Mike Hussey, who turned down singles to keep the strike. My third point was that I thought that some of their batsmen were uncomfortable against our quick bowlers; even though it was only a one-day match, there were signs that there were little battles which we were winning.

I thought my remarks were quite measured but they produced a prickly response from Buchanan in reference to that final: 'What I saw yesterday was very, very encouraging from our point of view in terms of the way a lot of English players were dismissed, especially their top order,' he said. 'It would be interesting for him [Fletcher] to reflect on how Trescothick has got out, how Strauss has got out, how Vaughan has got out through the course of the series so far with the Test matches in mind. I just don't think we've really exposed the weaknesses of the English team at the moment as well as we should have done,' he continued. 'That's partly a credit to England – Flintoff's bowled well, Harmison's bowled some good balls and they've had some support at times . . . But I think they've got three fieldsmen only. Collingwood is obviously a very good fieldsman; Solanki, who they bring on, Pietersen is quick to the ball . . . but other than that I think they are quite lumbering in the field.' This was a man under pressure. That was clear; it would soon become even clearer.

Now we had to play the NatWest Challenge – three more one-day matches which were always going to be tricky because of the inevitable 'After the Lord Mayor's show' feeling, although added interest came in the form of the new regulations governing the so-called supersubs and powerplays. For the uninitiated this meant that a team could bring on a football-style substitute (nominated before the toss) at any stage of the match. As for the powerplays, they meant that the fielding restrictions would compulsorily be in place for the first ten overs, and then there would be two blocks of five overs which could be used whenever the fielding captain wished. The supersub principle resulted in the call-up of Sussex's Matt Prior to replace Worcestershire's Kabir Ali, because we felt that Prior, whom we had seen when he made his international one-day debut in Zimbabwe, could add something; not just because his batting is generally aggressive but also because he can be flexible in being able to bat anywhere in the order. Even though he is a wicketkeeper, he is also a very agile fielder, too.

My worry with these two innovations was that they were being tried at the same time. How could you know which one was working and which one was not? How much effect was one having as opposed to the other? I also thought they should have been trialled at a lower level somewhere. The international arena should not be used as a practice area for this sort of thing.

What actually happened with the supersub scenario was that

the toss became even more important than it already is – which is very important in England on seaming pitches. It would make a great deal more sense if the captains were allowed to name their substitutes after the toss has been made. This was suggested to the ICC after this tournament but was turned down.

As for the powerplays, the matches we played did not really show any possible effects, because they were just used up-front in the first twenty overs and that was that. But they do interest me and I would like to see how they fare in other countries, especially the sub-continent.

I felt that it was going to be difficult to pick the players up after the Lord's final, so was pleasantly surprised when things went so well in the first match at Headingley. To beat Australia by nine wickets in any sort of match is some achievement. And it was not an easy day once we had heard about the terrible London bombings. That news filtered through just after we had warmed up. It made the dressing room a quiet and sombre place, but I thought the players did well to concentrate on the cricket when they had to. You cannot put something as awful as that completely out of your mind, and the television was on in the dressing room so that everyone could keep abreast of developments. Naturally thoughts soon turned to whether the two last matches in this Challenge would go ahead in London. But that was not a decision for us, but for the administrators.

It was said that the toss was vitally important. It was important, yes, but probably less so than it was at Lord's in the next game. What was crucial was that we bowled well at Headingley, and we did so after a sticky start. Sticky, because the bowlers struggled with their footing at the outset and so produced some pretty ordinary stuff. But they settled and it was a good performance. Simon Jones bowled especially well even though he did not take a wicket. It is easy to forget how inexperienced he is in one-day cricket. Even now, at the end of the 2005 season, he has only played twenty-one one-day matches – for any team at the professional level. If he can stay fit, though, he will play many more.

Collingwood picked up four wickets, but for me the dominance and ruthlessness of the top three batsmen was the most impressive aspect. In days gone by we might have won that match with eight wickets down but we took control, especially Trescothick – his 104 not out being his first century against Australia – and Vaughan (59 not out). Not a bad riposte to Mr Buchanan, who now became rather desperate in his behaviour.

The second match was back at Lord's. Now, it had always been the case in the past that England were the first team to the ground. In fact many times I had heard Australians mocking us for our insistence on being there so early. But now all of a sudden the Australians were there before us. And not only that, they decided to book the space on the outfield where they knew that we always practised – that is to say, the top half of the ground. As I said, it seemed that Buchanan was becoming desperate with this example of one-upmanship. We just laughed it off and went to practise on the lower half of the ground. The Australians won that game but it was nothing to do with that. In fact I came away from that day feeling pretty confident that there had been shifts in the psychological battle, which we had not seen previously.

Having lost the toss I thought we did well to get to 223–8, because it was seaming around a lot. Flintoff scored 87 which signalled a return to some semblance of form with the bat for him and it showed that we had made progress in the one-day game, because in years gone by we would probably have been all out for something like 180 in 46 overs. At least we set them something competitive, but the pitch flattened out and they knocked the required runs off for the loss of just three wickets, with Ricky Ponting scoring a good hundred.

We lost the toss again at The Oval and could not post a decent enough total despite Pietersen giving a further demonstration of his talent and gumption in making 74. Supersub Solanki also made 53 not out, which made it an interesting day for Simon Jones, who was named in the starting line-up and then replaced without doing anything else. There are a few fast bowlers I know who would long to have that sort of workload every day!

Adam Gilchrist smashed 121 not out so that Australia won by eight wickets. That spawned a lot of negativity – outside of the team at least. 'Those last two games are a precursor to the rest of the summer,' the sceptics were saying. There was much focus on the top order batting and how they had supposedly been found out by the Australians. That did not overly concern me. In fact if we go back to that ICC game in 2004 and also include the Twenty20 match, I make it that we were one up on the Australians in all those one-day matches: 4–3 to us. That would do nicely for me, thank you very much. We had shown that we could compete with them on given days. I was happy with that. It was time for the Ashes.

# 3

There was a small matter which had bothered me about the last two matches in the NatWest Challenge. We had been too nice. Too familiar. The 'get in their space' attitude had suddenly begun to dissipate a little, amid the obvious respect which the Australians were showing us. When Ricky Ponting scored his hundred at Lord's, a couple of our players made a special point of walking across and shaking his hand. There was no need to do that. Of course, you can congratulate him. If you are standing next to him you might shake his hand; if further away, maybe clap your hands and shout 'well played'. But I felt that was being over-friendly because it was too pointed a signal of congratulation. There were some very good examples of sportsmanship later in the series. Andrew Flintoff shaking Brett Lee's hand at the end of the Edgbaston Test was a magnificent gesture – one of the moments of the series – but it was after the battle was won. It is different then. England teams have to be careful, especially the bowlers, because they can easily lose their focus when their behaviour becomes too matey on the field. And that is what we did in those last two one-day matches. We were much less aggressive; Glenn McGrath had picked that up and mentioned it in an interview. He was right. We had to rediscover that edge before the First Test at Lord's. OK, the players were always going to be up for it in such an eagerly anticipated encounter, but that energy had to be channelled in the appropriate areas. We were going to go flat out at them; no holds barred.

First, though, the selectors had to pick the team. No easy task. Of course there was only one place about which there was any doubt; the same number five spot which had caused all that debate before the Bangladesh Tests. It was Thorpe versus Pietersen, round two. Some people still considered Ian Bell to be in the shake-up, but for those reasons outlined earlier, he was not. We did not feel comfortable with either Thorpe or Pietersen batting at number four. It was a straight choice between the pair for the number five position.

It was one of the most difficult decisions in which I had been involved in my time with England. It truly was 50/50. We ummed and aahed for a long time. There were, though, a few things nagging at the back of my mind. First, I thought that I had seen signs during the winter in South Africa that Thorpe's appetite for the game was waning. I have always liked him as a fellow and as a player – nuggety, solid and reliable. And I would like to think that I was tolerant and sympathetic towards him when he had those well-publicised personal problems. I remember being in Sri Lanka for the ICC Champions Trophy in 2002 when Nasser Hussain handed me his mobile phone. 'It's Thorpey,' he said with a look on his face which told me that it was going to be bad news. After considerable problems that summer Thorpe had declared himself available for the Ashes tour on which we were about to embark, but now he was telling me that he had changed his mind. It was a serious blow.

The second concern I had was that I thought that if we were going to beat the Australians we were going to have to attack them. To do that we would need someone at number five who could really dominate; an imposing, boisterous figure. Thorpe could do many things but he could not fit that mould. And not just with his batting. His character was such that he was one of the quiet guys in the changing room. I am not saying that he was not a tough character – he undoubtedly is – but he just used to get on with his job. You could argue that Bell is a very similar character – also very quiet – but he had done so well in his Test career so far. His debut against the West Indies at The Oval in 2004 had been impressive, and he had continued that against the admittedly weaker Bangladesh. He had youth on his side as well, of course, and had been scoring heavily for Warwickshire. He had to play.

There was still much vacillation. I phoned people like Mike Atherton and Nasser Hussain whose opinions I value and respect greatly, and they thought that we should pick Thorpe. That confused me even more. Consideration also had to be given to the fact that Shane Warne was likely to be more troublesome to the left-handers than the right-handers. Pitching in the rough outside their off-stump was going to cause problems. This much was proved later in the series. 'Would Thorpe be able to cope with this?' I asked myself. Warne was probably going to be bowling when he came to the wicket – never an easy proposition for any batsman. Even the highest quality players will tell you that they prefer to face some seam before spin.

The final thing which was troubling me about Thorpe was that I knew that he needed a lot of batting. He was not the type of player who could just waltz back into the game after a break and be fluent immediately. He needed runs and time in the middle behind him. He just did not have them at this stage. Since the Second Test against Bangladesh he had played just five innings (one of those a duck for Surrey's second eleven), having endured a series of injections – one an epidural – in an effort to shake off a chronic back complaint. In his last game before we met to select the Ashes twelve he had scored 73 against Gloucestershire but the reports we received were that it was on a very flat pitch against an unthreatening attack; that Thorpe had not been quite as dominant as we might have liked.

It was, though, that last concern which kept coming back to me – Thorpe had not played enough cricket to be in the sort of shape required against the Australians. That eventually swung it for me – allied, of course, to the fact that Pietersen was scoring lots of runs by then. Pietersen it was to be.

Usually when such a big decision is made, it is a relief. I can normally walk away and virtually forget about it. But not this one. I could not stop thinking about it. Had we done the right thing? Even right up until the start of the First Test at Lord's I was thinking about that. Most of my cricketing friends I spoke

1. Michael Vaughan with his opposite number Ricky Ponting, at the toss before the first day of the First Test at Lord's. Vaughan lost this and the toss at Edgbaston, but thanks to a curious call by Ponting there, we were able to bat first in all but this opening Test.

The series began with a rip-roaring day at Lord's, with seventeen wickets falling. Here's Matthew Hoggard taking the first, bowling opener Matthew Hayden for 12. Hayden had a rid time all through the series until his 138 at The Oval.

3. Steve Harmison celebrates his dismissal of Jason Gillespie, lbw for 1, in returning his best figures for the series in this innings: 5 for 43.

4. Sharing a joke with Ashley Giles during a training session at Lord's.

5. Kevin Pietersen offered brilliant resistance in his maiden Test fifty on his debut. It took an outstanding catch by Damien Martyn on the boundary to dismiss him.

An early breakthrough in Australia's second innings as Pietersen runs out Langer for 6.

7. From left to right: Andrew Strauss, Andrew Flintoff and Marcus Trescothick appeal successfully for the wicket of Michael Clarke.

8. Another run-out: this time it's Brett Lee who goes, thanks to a direct hit by Ashley Gile

9. Pietersen battled valiantly again for his second Test fifty but was left stranded as we were all out for 180.

Shane Warne (in white hat) celebrates catching Simon Jones off McGrath to give Australia victory by 239 runs in the First Test.

# SECOND TEST, EDGBASTON

11. Our hopes of squaring the series in the Second Test at Edgbaston got an undeniable boost with the news that McGrath had been injured in a freak accident during a pre-match warm-up. He would be replaced by paceman Michael Kasprowicz.

12. Trescothick and Strauss (right) shake hands on reaching their hundred partnership in England's first innings. Ponting's decision to put us in backfired as we piled on 407 on the first day.

13. Trescothick clumps Warne for four during his first-innings knock of 90.

14. Andrew Flintoff gets in on the action, enjoying one of his five sixes on the way to 68.

15. Flintoff and Brett Lee congratulate each other after an epic contest.

16. England's fielders await a decision on a run-out from the TV umpire. From left to right Geraint Jones, Andrew Strauss, Michael Vaughan, Marcus Trescothick, Kevin Pietersen and Andrew Flintoff.

to, I asked, 'What would you have done?' The answers were split.

I phoned Thorpe. His attitude was outstanding. He was very mature about the decision. He even said to me, 'Duncan, you know what? If I had been a selector I would have done the same. I think you've made the right decision.' I gave him the benefit of my advice. I said, 'Look, if you are still keen to play then go and get some hundreds to prove us wrong. Maybe we have made a mistake and you can force your way back into the side. There could still be a dream ending for you at The Oval to go out on a high.' He was fine about it. I honestly did not think that he was going to retire, judging by that conversation. The next thing I knew, he had, which was sad.

It is so hard making a decision like that. It is without doubt the worst part of my job. Just think about how often other people in other walks of life have to do that. Of course, it happens in business, but with people you get to know as closely as I do with the England cricketers? I doubt it. For I do develop a close relationship with them, a bond which has occurred more readily since we have achieved such consistency in our selection. They become good friends whom I really get to know as individuals. Then suddenly they have to be told: 'Sorry, you're not playing.' And in this case it meant the end of a player's career. It must also be hard for the other selectors, David Graveney and Geoff Miller.

But the choice had been made, and it was time to prepare for the First Test. In dealing with the squad's preparation for that match – and every other Test – it is probably best if I give you an insight into the way I like my cricket teams to be organised; the structure I like to put in place so that the team can perform to its optimum.

I consider myself the consultant to the cricket team. That is derived from my business background. Every team I have been involved in has had the same team management structure. The captain is always the boss – the managing director – and below him is a middle management team (made up of players and distinct from my administrative management team, which has a very different role) which is consulted for advice on all core decisions. I discovered that the captain must be the boss when I became skipper of Zimbabwe in the early 1980s. Being an all-rounder, I was worried that I might not be able to spend as much time on my own game as I wanted, so I asked for an omnipotent coach to be appointed. He was Peter Carlstein, the former Rhodesian batsman who played eight Tests for South Africa and is now settled in Australia, but within five or six net sessions I realised that there was a serious problem, because nobody knew who was in charge. The players cannot have two bosses and this was how they felt here. It was an important lesson which has stood me in good stead ever since.

The management team usually consists of three or four players from differing parts of the squad – for example a batsman, a bowler and a youngster – who can give the captain and coach a feel of the mood in the camp. They are the equivalents of your floor managers, sales managers and works managers in business. I think that this arrangement covers all the bases in leadership terms, because it usually ensures that the correct decisions are made. I have been involved in teams with an average leader but a strong management team, which have nearly always prospered, and also those with an outstanding leader backed up with an average management team, which have not usually been so successful. Ideally you obviously want an outstanding leader backed up by an outstanding management team. That is what we have got with England at the moment. Some players might feel uncomfortable speaking directly to the captain or coach about a certain issue, but instead might be able to pour their heart out to a member of the management team, who can then relay the message to the captain and coach.

Being on the management team brings with it a measure of honour and responsibility too. Players usually respond positively to being invited on to it. I don't know too many people who do not enjoy being bestowed with some responsibility. Funnily enough Thorpe is a good example. Apparently in the past he was something of a rebel, not particularly caring for punctuality or dress code, but once involved in the decision-making for such protocol he was happy to be responsible for areas which had previously irritated him. Phil Tufnell and Andrew Caddick were other examples of players who might have been seen as previously 'awkward' characters, but who responded well to being asked on to this group.

So for the Ashes Tests that management group comprised Michael Vaughan, Andrew Flintoff, Andrew Strauss and Marcus Trescothick. For the preceding one-day series the only change had been that Darren Gough was on it instead of Strauss. The group actually changes quite regularly because Ashley Giles was on it not so long ago as well. But Flintoff represented the bowlers, Trescothick the batsmen and Strauss played probably the most important role by being the new boy whom a lot of people could speak to if they had concerns.

This group will always decide upon matters such as discipline and dress codes. I have always been a stickler for such things. I think that they matter. I do not care what the uniform is – whether it is trendy or old-fashioned – as long as everyone wears the same, down to the smallest detail. Shirt and tie with a blazer used to be the norm, but I do not think that always necessary now – a tasteful polo shirt can look just as smart. But, of course, I recognise that there are times when a blazer needs to be worn. Certain dinners and arrivals in a country for the start of a tour are examples of when they need to be on show as a mark of respect.

When I first became coach of England in 1999 I was amazed that I was given a blazer which was exactly the same in appearance as the one worn by the players. In that respect I did not think that I should have been seen as an equal of players like Hussain and Atherton. To play for your country is a huge honour, and I was very conscious of the fact that I had never played for England. It is a matter I have always borne in mind and it is now being changed – only a very subtle change in the badge, but one that is significant enough to identify a difference. Those who have played for England have the crown and three lions on their badge; those who have not have the coronet and three lions – which is the ECB's logo. Thus we will have the rather curious situation where one of my assistants, Matthew

Maynard, will have a 'better' blazer than me, but I think that is only right. He played for England. I did not.

The same principle will hopefully apply to the caps of those who have not actually played Test cricket for England. For instance a player might be selected for a tour but might not make the Test side – what sort of cap does he wear? In my opinion he should not have a cap like the others who have represented England in Test matches. A good example is Gloucestershire's Martyn Ball. He was called up for the tour of India in 2001 when Glamorgan's Robert Croft declined to tour after the terrible events of September 11. But he did not make the Test side. He had a cap like everyone else, though, because he played in a tour match. It was not his fault.

What happens when a substitute comes on to field? Don't worry; we will come to the issue of their use later. That did not erupt until the Fourth Test at Trent Bridge, remember. But when someone like Durham's Gary Pratt goes on to the field and it is sunny, what does he wear? That will be addressed if this subtle change is made. In fact at one stage during the summer, Warwickshire's Trevor Penney, who we used as an assistant fielding coach before he took up a post with Sri Lanka, went on to the field wearing a plain black cap.

There have been other minutiae which I have introduced to the kit which England players now wear. For instance the idea that players should be awarded special caps when they reach the various milestones of 25, 50, 75 and 100 caps for England – or even 125 in the case of Alec Stewart, the only England cricketer to have stretched that far (133 caps). That was an initiative I had begun when coaching at Western Province. I do not think that the England players will mind my saying that there was some indifference to this when it was first introduced. But they have come to like it. I thought that they would; I will always remember how proud Stewart and Atherton were to reach 100 caps together in the Test against the West Indies at Old Trafford in 2000. So now it makes the others really proud to be presented with these caps, as Andrew Flintoff was on his home ground at Old Trafford, Ashley Giles was at The Oval for reaching 50 caps in the Ashes summer and indeed, Thorpe had been at Durham against Bangladesh when he reached 100 caps.

The same principle applies to the personalised numbers the players have on their shirts, signifying how many players have been capped by England before them. That gives them an identity as a Test player (making sure that their shirts differ from the replicas worn by fans) and makes them proud.

I am also delighted that the players now receive mementoes, sponsored by Vodafone, for their good performances in international cricket. So for centuries and five-wicket hauls they are presented with gleaming solid silver bats (about nine inches high) and balls mounted on wooden plinths. The wicketkeeper will also receive solid silver keeping gloves if he takes five catches. As yet no fielder has taken five catches but if he does, he will probably receive a ball too. For winter performances the players usually receive these special keepsakes at the Vodafone dinner at the start of the summer, but we also make some presentations after that. We invite legends of the game, such as Richie Benaud, Ian Botham, David Gower, Atherton, Nasser Hussain and

Michael Holding to come in and make the presentations before play on a given Test match day.

When the team management group meets, the assistant coaches Maynard and Troy Cooley will sit in as well, as will Phil Neale who, as operations manager, will just deal with such administrative housekeeping as tickets, car parking at grounds, and so on. Analyst Tim Boon will also be present, having video footage of the opposition ready to use on the projector screen, so that we can formulate batting and bowling plans.

As I said, this group will discuss a variety of things. Sometimes it might talk about the composition and length of practice sessions. It might deliberate the make-up of the eleven for a match – although Vaughan and I will always take the final decision on that, usually at practice on the day before the Test or on the morning of the match if there is bad weather about. It might talk of whether we should bat or bowl if we win the toss. It is important that it mulls over such an array of topics. You just never know; somebody might just come up with a great idea which no one else has thought of.

Of course, this does not mean that the rest of the team are excluded. At the first practice before a Test – usually on the Tuesday afternoon after we have convened on the Monday evening – I like to sit the team down on the square, near the pitch on which they will be playing. We will talk. As we do so, the players can familiarise themselves with the ground on which they are to play. If it is not the first Test of a series we will discuss what happened in the previous Test; what went right and if things did go wrong, what we can do to improve. But in that chat, I often tell those on the team management group to keep quiet, otherwise they might end up dominating the discussion. That way we should get to hear everyone's opinion over the course of time. That creates a joint team effort, where everyone is involved in that decision-making process. It is no use if you have a team sitting around waiting for one person to make a decision. Then it is easy for the team to use that person's judgement as a crutch should they fail. 'I was told to do that,' they might weakly protest. Not with this method.

Every player also has a copy of this poem:

When you get what you want in your struggle for self
And the world makes you king for a day,
Just go to the mirror and look at yourself
And see what that man has to say.

For it isn't your father or mother or wife
Whose judgment upon you must pass
The fellow whose verdict counts most in your life
Is the one staring back from the glass.

You may be like Jack Horner and chisel a plum
And think you're a wonderful guy.
But the man in the glass says you're only a bum
If you can't look him straight in the eye.

He's the fellow to please – never mind all the rest,
For he's with you clear to the end.

And you've passed your most dangerous, difficult test
If the man in the glass is your friend.

You may fool the whole world down the pathway of years
And get pats on the back as you pass.
But your final reward will be heartache and tears
If you've cheated the man in the glass.

'The Man in the Glass' by Dale Wimbrow (1895–1954)

It is a vital part of our approach to cricket. 'Look in the mirror' is a constant refrain when any complaining might arise. Everyone has responsibility and they must accept that.

A good example occurred on our one-day tour to Zimbabwe with a young side in 2001. In the net sessions before the matches got under way I really wanted the players to think about what they were attempting to do in that practice, rather than just turn up and go through the motions. So I decided that I would start questioning players before we started so that they would be thinking beforehand about what they wanted to do. The intention was to shock them a little by suddenly throwing questions at them about their practice method. However, the first time I tried this, I did not want to embarrass anyone, so I primed Graham Thorpe that I was going to ask him (supposedly suddenly) at the first practice. But the effect was still there. The younger players were made to think: 'Hang on, even a really senior player like Thorpey is being picked on here. I'd better start thinking about this.' And Thorpe made some excellent points, which was of considerable benefit to all concerned. It made him feel important and included him in the decision-making process, as well as alerting the rest to the fact that they would be called on too.

The management group will meet at 6 p.m. on the night before a Test. The whole team are then called in for a meeting afterwards. At that first meeting Tim Boon will show a video of all the opposition's bowlers running up to bowl so that our batsmen can visualise them; and also all their batsmen getting out so that the bowlers can do the same. That is mostly technical, but at the end of the meeting he will also show a motivational package put together to some tunes which are provided by Ashley Giles's music system. In it will be clips of all our batsmen striking fours and sixes, and of all the opposition batsmen being dismissed. It is always a great way – tremendously uplifting – for the players to leave the room.

The preparation for the first Ashes Test had begun on Monday, 18 July 2005. Or rather that was when we met up. The preparation had probably begun before that ICC Champions Trophy match at Edgbaston in 2004, to which I keep referring. It was before that when Boon had shown me the detailed video analysis of the Australian players. Not much had changed – either in personnel or technique – since then. We had made some good plans then, so were happy that they did not need too much tinkering. But it was at Lord's on that Monday lunchtime that we sat down and went through them in detail. Much was made throughout the summer of how good our plans were, but in truth they were little different from those we have made before. They just required some fine-tuning.

I will tell you a strange story. Remember Brisbane in 2002?

When Nasser Hussain famously won the toss and fielded? Australia scored 492 and we ended up losing by 384 runs. Ah, that decision. Generally, I am a 'bat first' man, but there were mitigating circumstances here, and I can say in all honesty that I agreed that we should bowl first. Indeed in the post-match press conference, I unequivocally said that. 'Did you support the captain?' I was asked. 'Yes, I did,' I replied emphatically. I did not skirt around the issue, as some coaches might have. I remember Scyld Berry of the *Sunday Telegraph* coming up afterwards and praising me for that. He seemed to be implying that quite a few of the other pressmen had been impressed by that too.

Many of the other senior players agreed with the decision and I think it is opportune that I should allow you to read these words: 'Brisbane – if there is to be any lateral movement off the seam it will be on day one. However, the pitch is generally slow on the first day and the bounce tennis ball-like. The best days for batting are two, three and four. It has turned towards the end of the match in recent years but is by no means a raging turner.'

Rod Marsh wrote those words. We had asked him to give us an appraisal of every pitch and what we might expect. I am not totally blaming him for that decision. But it is undeniable that his comments were a small contributory factor. When we had first seen the pitch, it was green, so we already had mixed feelings then, especially with the inexperienced bowling attack which we had. Of course, with the benefit of that wonderful thing – hindsight – we were wrong, but everything seemed to be telling us that if there was going to be an occasion to bowl first, then this was it. It was some consolation that when we met up with

Matthew Elliott later on that tour, when he appeared for Australia A against us, he said: 'That pitch at Brisbane always confuses us. Whenever I play for Victoria there, we never know whether to bat or bowl first.'

But the odd thing was that in that Brisbane Test only one of the Australian batsmen was not dismissed according to the plans we had devised and agreed upon. That was Ricky Ponting, who was somewhat bizarrely bowled around his legs by Giles off his thigh pad. All the rest fell as we wanted. 'But how come they scored so many?' I can hear you ask – and you have every justification in doing so. Well, one reason was that Simon Jones suffered his horrific knee injury and we were a bowler short from just after lunch on that first day; a fact that is often overlooked when poor old Hussain is receiving a hammering for his decision. The other reason is that we did not bowl enough balls in the right place. Plans to dismiss a batsman do not work unless you can bowl five or six balls an over in that area. That is what Australia's bowlers have been doing to our batsmen for years. It was time for them to take some of their own medicine in the summer of 2005.

Things could hardly have gone smoother on that front. Usually you have to have a plan B as well as a plan A for every batsman, but during this Ashes series we barely had to venture beyond that plan A. I do not want to go into elaborate detail about the plans for every batsman, because it will not be long before we play the Australians again, and why should I let them all know what we are thinking?

But there were only two batsmen for whom we made minor

alterations during the course of the summer, and one of them was Shane Warne, who was to surprise us a little with his batting. Our initial plan was to bounce him out, but after this First Test at Lord's, that became difficult because of the slowness of the pitches. Warne befuddled our bowlers by moving about the crease. Sometimes he would move right across his stumps (that would prove his downfall here at Lord's, when Steve Harmison would bowl him behind his legs) but on other occasions he would stay inside the line of the ball and carve away on the off-side – that is his real strength. Often it was as if he was putting himself inside the mind of the bowler and predicting what he might do. This is when a bowler then has to think like a batsman and counteract that. Nothing is black and white in any plan. Subtle changes are sometimes required. We eventually resolved just to bowl straight at middle stump to Warne and to forget about his messing around at the crease.

Michael Clarke was the other one. For him we thought that it was crucial that we stopped him scoring boundaries early on. Any batsman craves boundaries early on but he was especially reliant on them for sustenance amid his nervous energy. His favourite scoring area is on the leg-side and we thought that we could trap him lbw using a conventional field with a squarish mid-wicket. We were not convinced that he liked the short ball either; plenty of bouncers with a short leg and maybe a leg gully might be an option if the pitch allowed. But later we detected an interesting technical aspect to his batting, in that, unusually, he splays his front foot open when driving on the leg-side. That is to say that his toes are pointing down the pitch (maybe even towards the leg-side) rather than towards extra cover, as is the case with most batsmen. It means that he does not hit across his front pad, as we first thought. But what it does mean is that he squares himself up when playing off the back foot on the off-side. We therefore decided to redirect our energies in that area. We could always still catch him unawares and go for the lbw as well by placing a very straight mid-wicket (allowing mid-on to go a little deeper). With that blocked off we fancied that he would aim squarer and hit across the line.

Much was made during the summer of the specific field placings employed against the Australians. The credit for those must go to Michael Vaughan. We talk about the strategies for each batsman and then he formulates the field placings which will facilitate them. The field used for Matthew Hayden was one which provoked much comment and analysis, with one man positioned very straight on the drive (almost standing on the cut strip on the off-side) and another close in at cover, exactly where Andrew Strauss caught him first ball at Edgbaston off Matthew Hoggard. In fact we had used the straight man before, but it was Vaughan's clever idea to position the second man squarer.

Another idea was sampled before this First Test. For at Lord's we had a special visitor. The name of Alan Chambers might not mean that much to you. It certainly did not to me beforehand. But what a remarkable man, and what a remarkable story he had to tell us. For in 2000 he and fellow Royal Marine commando Charlie Paton became the first Britons to reach the geographical North Pole without support, dragging their 250lb sledges

500 miles across the ice from Canada. Their party had begun as four but two others pulled out, one through exhaustion and the other through frostbite, as Chambers and Paton survived temperatures as low as −30°C on as little as half a cup of porridge a day. The day before they reached the Pole and raised the Union flag on top of the world, they ran out of food. Chambers was subsequently awarded the MBE for his determination and strong leadership in the worst polar weather for twenty years.

It was some story. It could easily be said that we lost the Test after we heard it, and that it had no effect. But it did have an effect. Long into the Test series, there were still calls of 'Remember the Iceman' being heard in the dressing room. He told us one story of how they were on an iceberg which was drifting away from the main ice tract and of their battle to get back on track. We used that analogy after we lost this Test at Lord's.

But I am getting ahead of myself. Let us deal with that First Test. The first thing to say is that it began pretty well. Dismissing the Australians for 190 on the opening day of a Test match is not to be sniffed at. I was delighted with the attitude too. That aggression was back. In the team-talk we had made a special point of going at the Australians – 'get in their space' was the key phrase again. Vaughan then made a marvellous decision (one of many he was to make in this series) by deciding to opt for Steve Harmison to bowl the first over of the day. That role had always fallen to Hoggard before, but, by his own admission, his ducking swingers lack the naked hostility of Harmison's thunderbolts. Their purposes are rather different. So when Justin Langer was struck on the elbow by Harmison's second ball, the Australians will have known what our intentions were in this series. If they did not recognise this immediately, then they will have done so when both Hayden and Ponting were hit on the head soon afterwards by Harmison, who went on to claim his sixth five-for in Tests.

It was cricket in the raw that first morning. I really enjoyed it, but did we bowl a little too short, too often? Maybe. But we were pumped up; we were attacking. You could easily look back with the benefit of hindsight and say that they scored too many on that first day, but we were happy coming off the field, having bowled them out so cheaply.

But it was then that we realised how bowler-friendly this pitch was, especially when bowlers were operating from the Pavilion End. Seventeen wickets fell on the first day; fourteen of them from that end. Glenn McGrath bowled superbly – taking his 500th Test wicket when dismissing Marcus Trescothick – but everything was in his favour; the slope and the uneven bounce from that end played right into his hands. We were grateful for a partnership of 58 between Kevin Pietersen and Geraint Jones and some gutsy lower-order (never call them the tail) efforts which saw us to within 35 of the Australians. We were 92–7 overnight and made it our goal in our morning team-talk to make another 50 on the second morning, so to have made another 63 was pleasing.

It was a relief that Pietersen immediately produced on his debut. As I said, I had still been worrying right up to the start of the match about whether we had made the correct decision. If he had made nought, there are any number of critics out there who would have been all too pleased to have an opportunity to carp. Instead they turned their attention to the tyro Ian Bell, especially when he showed some inexperience in the second innings by padding up to Shane Warne to be lbw. It turned out to be a 'slider' which went straight on but it looked to most like that it was going to be a leg-break. But still Bell was probably a little naïve in looking to leave a ball like that which was pitching on the stumps. A more seasoned international batsman might have looked to play that with his pad, while trying to make it look as if he was playing a shot. Mind you, that would only have resulted in Warne bellowing in the umpire's ear.

The Australians got away from us in their second innings when Michael Clarke and Damien Martyn were putting on 155 for the fourth wicket. That was the partnership which really killed us off. There were, of course, dropped catches, none more highlighted than Pietersen's drop of Clarke off Simon Jones at extra cover, when the Australian had made only 21. He went on to make 91. It was Pietersen's third drop in two days, which surprised me. He had fielded well in the one-day series. It was only later in the series that I picked up a slight technical flaw, but generally it can be put down to over-eagerness. That is the way he is. He is always rushing around at 100mph. But you know what the good thing about him is? It was a character trait which I picked up on immediately when he was playing his early one-day internationals in Zimbabwe last winter. There in Bulawayo he made nought and dropped a sitter of a catch early on, but he never let his head go down. The very next ball he was clapping his hands and encouraging the rest of the team. He will never sulk in the field and that takes a special character to be able to behave like that after a mistake.

Geraint Jones is the same in that respect. He dropped a couple at the end of their second innings but they were not that costly. Sometimes when a team goes out to bat after fluffing a few chances at the end of the opposition's innings, confidence can be affected, because a bad tone has been set. But that was not the case here. Trescothick and Andrew Strauss actually gave us a decent start in the second innings, putting on 80 before Warne began to cause problems. At least that day we played McGrath much better, having had a long chat about playing him after the first innings – which was to have ramifications later in the series. But by the end of play on Saturday we were five wickets down and the game was up. There was heavy rain on the Sunday morning but once play started, it took just 61 balls for the Australians to finish the game. McGrath turned his devastation of the top order in the first innings to the lower order, snatching four wickets for three runs in just 23 balls, leaving Pietersen to play a brave lone hand, ending with 64 not out. Well done the selectors, we had got something right, but the flip side was that we were all out for 180 and had lost by 239 runs. That is a hammering, and there was no escaping that fact. But there was also no excuse for the waves of negativity and depression which engulfed the country. We were written off immediately.

It was a stressful time for me and the team, but I can honestly say that I always retained my belief in them throughout this period. Nobody outside that squad gave us a prayer of being able to recover. But I knew that we could. That is why I was so adamant that there should be no changes. Predictably there were widespread calls for that to be the case. But I knew that we had to remain strong in our belief in this team. All those victories over the previous couple of years and all the advances we had made could not be forgotten because of one bad performance. Because that is all that it was in my eyes; we had played poorly in one game. It was not a case of my saying to myself, 'Oh my God, we are never going to beat this lot. They are miles better than us.' Far from it.

I know that a lot of people smile dismissively when they hear a coach saying after a defeat, 'We've got to take the positives from this.' But it really was the case here. They were not empty platitudes when I said something similar. There was a good deal of encouragement to be drawn from that match. For a start we took twenty Australian wickets, and there were the individual performances of Harmison and Pietersen to applaud. Trescothick and Strauss gave us that solid start in the second innings too – that was important because there had been all that talk at the end of the one-day series that the Aussies had the wood on those two. For me one partnership (between Clarke and Martyn) turned the match. It would have been interesting to see how many we would have been chasing without that. Clutching at straws? I did not think so.

There is not much you can do in the immediate aftermath of such a defeat. I just told the players to go home and forget about it for a couple of days. They needed a break; it had been a draining Test match even if it did not go anywhere near the full distance. And it should not be forgotten that these players had been on the road all summer during the one-dayers.

There is little point in having a dressing-room inquest. I just do not think that they are advisable in such circumstances. I did, though, speak to certain individuals to reassure them. Geraint Jones was one. I just wanted to stress to him how well he had batted and that he should not dwell on the dropped catches. Trescothick was another. Even though he had played well for his 44 in the second innings, he was worried about his technique. I told him that I could see nothing wrong.

Any concern I had centred upon Vaughan and Flintoff, both of whom had struggled with the bat, Vaughan making just 3 and 4 and Flintoff 0 and 3. My worry was that I fancied these to be such important individuals in the series. Vaughan had made all those runs before against Australia and I knew that Flintoff could inflict real damage upon them. This had been his first Test against them and it had come to my attention that there were some disparaging noises coming out of their camp about him. 'Scared of fast bowling' was one of them. Huh, we would see about that.

As is usual when there is something of a break after a Test match, I now had a decision to make about how much cricket the players could participate in for their counties before the next Test. Since central contracts were introduced – the single most important change for the betterment of English cricket, in my opinion – there has always been controversy about these decisions. There is so much parochialism and short-sightedness that it is scarcely credible. You would hope that everyone would be more concerned about the welfare of the England team rather than of a particular county team, but so often that is not the case.

My biggest gripe is that too often my reasons for withdrawing players are misunderstood. Resting players between Test matches is more about mental relaxation than physical. And so that was uppermost in my thoughts here as I determined how much each player should play. There was not that much four-day county championship cricket available to the players anyway, but it never entered my thinking that the players needed anything of that duration.

It was being said that the likes of Vaughan and Trescothick should have been playing for Yorkshire and Somerset against Derbyshire and Durham respectively in that form of the game. But that was the last thing I thought they required. Sitting around in another cricket dressing room for four days? It would only make them more stale.

People often forget that county coaches rest some of their players – mainly bowlers, obviously – during the season, but most of those cricketers are only playing for six months of the year. I am having to deal with cricketers who are playing all-year round. Imagine if we were on tour, having played a lot of cricket, and I did not rest one of the major players like Flintoff. I would be castigated. But because we are back in England, these very same people expect those very same players to appear in county matches. It is ludicrous.

It should also be remembered that when we play in England, we are still on tour. It is not as if we are sitting at home. If we play in Birmingham, Giles can stay at home; likewise, say, Vaughan in

Leeds and Flintoff in Manchester, but for the rest of the summer they are touring. Time at home with the family is limited. Wives and girlfriends can stay in team hotels but it is not quite the same.

I told Trescothick that he needed to go away and hit some balls in practice and then play in the Twenty20 Finals at The Oval. That would free him up, as it would Flintoff. And by coincidence both their counties progressed through the semi-finals to the final, which a young Somerset side, well led by South Africa's Graeme Smith, won. I watched that finals day on television.

I always try and watch as much county cricket as I can in that way. I find that that is the best way to do so, especially with the advances in technology these days. Sometimes, if time permits (which is rarely), I might go to a county ground, but even then I prefer to keep a low profile and watch on my own. I know that counties like to be hospitable and entertain me, but I find it difficult to watch the cricket properly if I am talking to county grandees. And too much of the time they will want to talk about their own players who might be seeking international recognition. That would only be natural, but it doesn't really help me in my quest to discover what I really want to know about any specific player.

A couple of the other players would play in one-day matches. Bell and Giles would play for Warwickshire against Kent (for whom Geraint Jones would appear) in a Totesport League match and Pietersen (who was still in the process of being placed on a central contract) against Worcestershire in the same competition, although that match was eventually rained off.

As for Vaughan, we decided between us that it would be best to spend some quality time in the nets again. It was something which we had done successfully before the West Indies Test at Lord's in 2004, and Vaughan went on to make two centuries in the match. He has never shied from hard work. In fact he always works his socks off, always putting in extra hours when others might be resting. So I said that I would go up to Leeds – the New Rover ground where Yorkshire's academy is situated – for two days for us to work together. Vaughan would then play in Yorkshire's Totesport League match against Kent on the Sunday, as would Hoggard, who would come to the nets to bowl too.

You may have heard of the term 'forward press'. It is a batsman's trigger movement by which I set great store, and whenever it is mentioned, Vaughan's name invariably crops up alongside. For it was on the Ashes tour in 2002/03 that he announced himself as a batsman of world-class quality, but also when he demonstrated that he had done considerable work in grooving a more pronounced forward press.

Without wishing to turn this into some sort of technical thesis, I think that I should explain. The basis of my theory about using this forward press is that I can see no reason why a batsman should not get into position early if he can. Why leave yourself to make a bigger movement when you can already be in position to make a shorter one? The old-fashioned coaches might argue that a batsman should stand still before delivery, but that is tosh – you cannot do that against the pace of bowler generally encountered today. To do so would also mean making a decision about where the ball is going to pitch almost at the same time as the ball is leaving the bowler's hand. And if you do that, you do not know if the ball is going to swing. But if you press, then you only have a small final movement to make to get to the pitch of the ball. So you can make your decision much later.

And, anyway, one of my major philosophies about batting is that the more movement you make, the greater the chance of error content. I favour a reasonably wide stance for a batsman, so that his press and then final movement do not have to be too large. How people's interpretation of this can be so wrong was emphasised to me on my first tour with England – to South Africa in 1999/2000. It occurred during the First Test at the Wanderers, on that damp pitch, if you remember, where we were reduced to 2–4 in the opening exchanges and soundly beaten by an innings and 21 runs. It was being said by all the commentators that the England batsmen had not got far enough forward when they were batting. 'Look at Herschelle Gibbs,' the commentators were saying. 'He is a good example to the English players. Watch how far forward he is getting.' Now I knew Gibbs well; I'd coached him as a youngster. I knew what he did. They were only judging him after he had played his shots. Yes, his front foot was a long way forward, but what they were not understanding was this: first, Gibbs has a wide stance; then when the bowler delivers the ball, he presses. So his last movement forward might only have been a couple of inches. I realised then that I had a lot of convincing to do about the forward press.

I also always emphasise that a batsman must make sure that his technique can look after him when he has made an error. That is what happens with the great batsmen. Their excellence is manifested in their technique getting them out of trouble when they make an error of judgement, rather than them playing shots more perfectly than others.

The press is not just a lunge forward, because sometimes it also involves a corresponding back foot movement to ensure that the batsman is aligned properly, in a position to hit the ball back where it comes from. It is important to get the timing of the initial movements right, though. You can, in fact, make them too early, but more likely is that you make them too late – and that is when it looks as if you are lunging. Commentators will say that a certain batsman is lunging on to the front foot too early, when in reality he is making the movement too late, and has no time to make the next movement. When Vaughan was struggling a little on the South African tour of 2004/05 it was because his timing of those trigger movements was slightly out. He is actually unusual in that he has always had a small third trigger movement with his front foot, and that was causing him slight problems.

Of course, when the England captain is not scoring too many runs, it leads to all sorts of enquiries and inquests among the pundits, but it did make me wonder when one of them, a very good South African Test batsman in his time (OK, it was Barry Richards), advised during that series: 'Michael Vaughan should go back to what he was doing in Australia a couple of winters ago – standing still before the ball is bowled.' Um, he'd obviously been watching carefully! There was no way Vaughan was standing still in Australia. He was doing exactly the same in South Africa as he had then. And we can always prove that, because by using the Feedback Analysis equipment, we keep footage of all the players when they were doing well, whether batting or bowling. That information is stored up to be used as an invaluable tool when a player is struggling.

So the inquests were beginning again now, especially as Vaughan had been bowled twice at Lord's. 'He's not moving his feet. His bat is not coming down straight, blah blah blah,' they all averred.

What was actually happening was that he was not quite getting his balance right when pressing forward. His weight was on the ball of his front foot, which is not ideal; rather it should be on the heel of that foot, bringing his centre of gravity back towards the leg-side. His centre of gravity was actually over towards the off-side, so his head was being dragged too far forward. When the third trigger movement then pulled him across a little, he could get his leg out of the way, but not his head, thus resulting in his playing inside out, exposing his stumps.

As for his bat not coming down straight, on most occasions when a ball seams back at you, you will come across the line. When it does seam, your bat is already on its way down – it has to be and you have to be assuming that the ball is going to go straight on – so that you now have to adjust. That is why it then looks as if you are playing across the line.

Sound complicated? It probably is. But it did not require huge modification. You cannot make big technical changes in between Tests anyway. Most trigger movements need to be instinctive. If you are thinking about them too much, you can get yourself in further trouble.

Vaughan was actually playing pretty well in my opinion. He

just needed to rediscover his original movements which had brought him so much success. Up in Leeds we varied the type of practice Vaughan did: facing Hoggard and other bowlers; using the bowling machine and also having throw-downs from me (no wonder I needed a shoulder operation recently!). At first all was not well. In fact at one stage he came out of the net in a fluster. He just could not get it right. 'Relax. Use your instinct. It will come,' I said.

It did. He was soon smashing the ball about without a care in the world. He scored 116 not out for Yorkshire against Kent in the Totesport League that Sunday.

# First Test

*England v. Australia*
*Lord's, London*
*21–24 July 2005*

**Umpires:** Aleem Dar (Pak) and R. Koertzen (SA)
**Toss:** Australia

| *Australia: 1st innings* | | | R | M | B | 4 | 6 |
|---|---|---|---|---|---|---|---|
| J. Langer | c Harmison | b Flintoff | 40 | 77 | 44 | 5 | 0 |
| M. Hayden | | b Hoggard | 12 | 38 | 25 | 2 | 0 |
| *R. Ponting | c Strauss | b Harmison | 9 | 38 | 18 | 1 | 0 |
| D. Martyn | c G. Jones | b S. Jones | 2 | 13 | 4 | 0 | 0 |
| M. Clarke | lbw | b S. Jones | 11 | 35 | 22 | 2 | 0 |
| S. Katich | c G. Jones | b Harmison | 27 | 107 | 67 | 5 | 0 |
| +A. Gilchrist | c G. Jones | b Flintoff | 26 | 30 | 19 | 6 | 0 |
| S. Warne | | b Harmison | 28 | 40 | 29 | 5 | 0 |
| B. Lee | c G. Jones | b Harmison | 3 | 13 | 8 | 0 | 0 |
| J. Gillespie | lbw | b Harmison | 1 | 19 | 11 | 0 | 0 |
| G. McGrath | not out | | 10 | 9 | 6 | 2 | 0 |
| Extras | (b 5, lb 4, w 1, nb 11) | | 21 | | | | |
| Total | (all out, 40.2 overs, 209 mins) | | 190 | | | | |

FoW: 1–35 (Hayden, 7.6 ov), 2–55 (Ponting, 12.5 ov), 3–66 (Langer, 14.4 ov), 4–66 (Martyn, 15.1 ov), 5–87 (Clarke, 21.5 ov), 6–126 (Gilchrist, 28.3 ov), 7–175 (Warne, 36.1 ov), 8–178 (Katich, 36.3 ov), 9–178 (Lee, 38.4 ov), 10–190 (Gillespie, 40.2 ov).

| *Bowling* | O | M | R | W |
|---|---|---|---|---|
| Harmison | 11.2 | 0 | 43 | 5 |
| Hoggard | 8 | 0 | 40 | 1 |
| Flintoff | 11 | 2 | 50 | 2 |
| S. Jones | 10 | 0 | 48 | 2 |

| England: 1st innings | | | R | M | B | 4 | 6 |
|---|---|---|---|---|---|---|---|
| M. Trescothick | c Langer | b McGrath | 4 | 24 | 17 | 1 | 0 |
| A. Strauss | c Warne | b McGrath | 2 | 28 | 21 | 0 | 0 |
| *M. Vaughan | | b McGrath | 3 | 29 | 20 | 0 | 0 |
| I. Bell | | b McGrath | 6 | 34 | 25 | 1 | 0 |
| K. Pietersen | c Martyn | b Warne | 57 | 148 | 89 | 8 | 2 |
| A. Flintoff | | b McGrath | 0 | 8 | 4 | 0 | 0 |
| +G. Jones | c Gilchrist | b Lee | 30 | 85 | 56 | 6 | 0 |
| A. Giles | c Gilchrist | b Lee | 11 | 14 | 13 | 2 | 0 |
| M. Hoggard | c Hayden | b Warne | 0 | 18 | 16 | 0 | 0 |
| S. Harmison | c Martyn | b Lee | 11 | 35 | 19 | 1 | 0 |
| S. Jones | not out | | 20 | 21 | 14 | 3 | 0 |
| Extras | (b 1, lb 5, nb 5) | | 11 | | | | |
| Total | (all out, 48.1 overs, 227 mins) | | 155 | | | | |

FoW: 1–10 (Trescothick, 6.1 ov), 2–11 (Strauss, 6.5 ov), 3–18 (Vaughan, 12.2 ov), 4–19 (Bell, 14.3 ov), 5–21 (Flintoff, 16.1 ov), 6–79 (G. Jones, 34.1 ov), 7–92 (Giles, 36.6 ov), 8–101 (Hoggard, 41.4 ov), 9–122 (Pietersen, 43.4 ov), 10–155 (Harmison, 48.1 ov).

| Bowling | O | M | R | W |
|---|---|---|---|---|
| McGrath | 18 | 5 | 53 | 5 |
| Lee | 15.1 | 5 | 47 | 3 |
| Gillespie | 8 | 1 | 30 | 0 |
| Warne | 7 | 2 | 19 | 2 |

| Australia: 2nd innings | | | R | M | B | 4 | 6 |
|---|---|---|---|---|---|---|---|
| J. Langer | run out (Pietersen) | | 6 | 24 | 15 | 1 | 0 |
| M. Hayden | | b Flintoff | 34 | 65 | 54 | 5 | 0 |
| *R. Ponting | c sub (Hildreth) | b Hoggard | 42 | 100 | 65 | 3 | 0 |
| D. Martyn | lbw | b Harmison | 65 | 215 | 138 | 8 | 0 |
| M. Clarke | | b Hoggard | 91 | 151 | 106 | 15 | 0 |
| S. Katich | c S. Jones | b Harmison | 67 | 177 | 113 | 8 | 0 |
| +A. Gilchrist | | b Flintoff | 10 | 26 | 14 | 1 | 0 |
| S. Warne | c Giles | b Harmison | 2 | 13 | 7 | 0 | 0 |
| B. Lee | run out (Giles) | | 8 | 16 | 16 | 1 | 0 |
| J. Gillespie | | b S. Jones | 13 | 72 | 52 | 3 | 0 |
| G. McGrath | not out | | 20 | 44 | 32 | 3 | 0 |
| Extras | (b 10, lb 8, nb 8) | | 26 | | | | |
| Total | (all out, 100.4 overs, 457 mins) | | 384 | | | | |

FoW: 1–18 (Langer, 5.3 ov), 2–54 (Hayden, 14.4 ov), 3–100 (Ponting, 27.3 ov), 4–255 (Clarke, 61.6 ov), 5–255 (Martyn, 62.1 ov), 6–274 (Gilchrist, 67.2 ov), 7–279 (Warne, 70.2 ov), 8–289 (Lee, 74.1 ov), 9–341 (Gillespie, 89.6 ov), 10–384 (Katich, 100.4 ov).

| Bowling | O | M | R | W |
|---|---|---|---|---|
| Harmison | 27.4 | 6 | 54 | 3 |
| Hoggard | 16 | 1 | 56 | 2 |
| Flintoff | 27 | 4 | 123 | 2 |
| S. Jones | 18 | 1 | 69 | 1 |
| Giles | 11 | 1 | 56 | 0 |
| Bell | 1 | 0 | 8 | 0 |

| England: 2nd innings (Target: 420 runs) | | | R | M | B | 4 | 6 |
|---|---|---|---|---|---|---|---|
| M. Trescothick | c Hayden | b Warne | 44 | 128 | 103 | 8 | 0 |
| A. Strauss | | c & b Lee | 37 | 115 | 67 | 6 | 0 |
| *M. Vaughan | | b Lee | 4 | 47 | 26 | 1 | 0 |
| I. Bell | lbw | b Warne | 8 | 18 | 15 | 0 | 0 |
| K. Pietersen | not out | | 64 | 120 | 79 | 6 | 2 |
| A. Flintoff | c Gilchrist | b Warne | 3 | 14 | 11 | 0 | 0 |
| +G. Jones | c Gillespie | b McGrath | 6 | 51 | 27 | 1 | 0 |
| A. Giles | c Hayden | b McGrath | 0 | 2 | 2 | 0 | 0 |
| M. Hoggard | lbw | b McGrath | 0 | 18 | 15 | 0 | 0 |
| S. Harmison | lbw | b Warne | 0 | 3 | 1 | 0 | 0 |
| S. Jones | c Warne | b McGrath | 0 | 12 | 6 | 0 | 0 |
| Extras | (b 6, lb 5, nb 3) | | 14 | | | | |
| Total | (all out, 58.1 overs, 268 mins) | | 180 | | | | |

FoW: 1–80 (Strauss, 26.3 ov), 2–96 (Trescothick, 29.2 ov), 3–104 (Bell, 33.1 ov), 4–112 (Vaughan, 36.2 ov), 5–119 (Flintoff, 39.3 ov), 6–158 (G. Jones, 50.3 ov), 7–158 (Giles, 50.5 ov), 8–164 (Hoggard, 54.6 ov), 9–167 (Harmison, 55.3 ov), 10–180 (S. Jones, 58.1 ov).

| Bowling | O | M | R | W |
|---|---|---|---|---|
| McGrath | 17.1 | 2 | 29 | 4 |
| Lee | 15 | 3 | 58 | 2 |
| Gillespie | 6 | 0 | 18 | 0 |
| Warne | 20 | 2 | 64 | 4 |

**Result:** Australia won by 239 runs
**Man of the Match:** G. McGrath
**Series:** Australia leads 1–0

# 4

Michael Vaughan was not done, though – we arranged to practise again at Edgbaston the morning after that hundred – and
neither were England. While we had worked in Leeds, we had
talked about that First Test at Lord's. And we were both adamant:
we had not been positive enough with our batting. We had
vowed to be so beforehand, but when it came to the crunch, we
had not been. We chatted especially about Shane Warne. We
needed to be more hungry for runs against him. The mindset of
the batsmen needed to be changed. Amid the players' natural
respect for him, they were playing too defensively and waiting for
the bad ball. The trouble with that method is that when the rare
bad ball does eventually arrive, you do not score off it. We
wanted to flip that mentality over, so that we looked to score off
every ball. Then if it was a good ball, we could defend it. You
cannot let such a great bowler dictate. We could not let any of
their bowlers dictate. But it was vital that the players knew that

they had the backing of the management to be positive. If they were out going hard at the Australians, they needed to know that there would be no recriminations; no mutterings of 'what an awful shot that was' should their positivity backfire.

By the end of the first day of the Second Test at Edgbaston we were all out for 407 in 79.2 overs, having hit 10 sixes and 54 fours. I think that it is fair to say that the message had been heard loud and clear.

But before we could reach that position of early dominance, there was much else to happen. Much else. First of all there was a furore in the press. As demonstrated by my already mentioned 'war of words' with John Buchanan, there was already plenty being said. Some England players were berated for making public comments about the series; especially Matthew Hoggard, who was supposed to have said that Glenn McGrath and Warne were past it. I'm not sure that he did actually say that, but it made a good story, and it ran and ran.

As someone who is not exactly overflowing with desire to make my innermost thoughts public, I had mixed feelings about all of this. But to a degree it did show that this England side was being positive. In the past if we did not say anything then we were accused of being timid. I have long known that you cannot really win these sorts of battles. However, what did upset me and the rest of the squad was the comment directed at Ashley Giles by Dave Houghton, a former Zimbabwean team-mate of mine, now coaching Derbyshire. After Giles's performance at Lord's – which even he himself would say was below par – Houghton said that England would be better off playing with ten men. What sort of comment is that? I know Houghton well and like him, and I wonder whether he was misinterpreted. If he was not, then I'm sure that he regrets saying that. It certainly hurt Giles a lot.

As did McGrath's comment that he thought the series score would 5–0. That made an impression on everyone within the squad. It was not a very clever comment by McGrath and I wonder what his team-mates made of it deep down. It was clearly an early attempt at public humiliation, but all it achieved was to spur our team on. Shrewd public comments can play mind games with some less secure players, but this, and some other remarks passed by the Australians, had gone beyond that. It was a strong motivating force for us.

When I arrived at Edgbaston on that Monday morning, there was growing concern that the weather might play a significant part in the Test. David Graveney had phoned on the Sunday to alert me as such. There had been torrential rain in Birmingham, with a tornado only just missing the ground. Three inches of rain had fallen in four days, leaving the covers floating on floodwater on the square. Groundsman Steve Rouse was not confident that he would be able to prepare the pitch in time. Already he was talking of a delayed start on Thursday, whatever the weather in the interim. It looked like the pitch would be a slow seamer. Giles might not play in such circumstances, especially if there was further rain and the game was reduced in duration. 'We'd better call up Colly,' I said to Vaughan. It was a logical decision to consider Paul Collingwood. It was not panic, as some suggested. To have picked him in the first place might have indicated panic. This was just common sense, because his bowling would be ideally suited to such a pitch and he could also add depth to our batting.

As it was, there was no further rain and everybody's worst fears about the pitch disappeared. By Tuesday it was already drying considerably and by Wednesday it was just like any other Edgbaston pitch. So we sent Collingwood back to play for Durham, to Southend in fact, where they were playing Essex.

There might also have been another reason for him to stay; Vaughan had been hit on the elbow on the Tuesday when facing Chris Tremlett in the nets. It looked quite nasty for a moment, with the captain in a good deal of pain. But I never doubted that he would play. He has shown time and time again that he is a tough cookie. He always wants to play, regardless of what might have happened, sometimes even regardless of what the medical people are telling him. I remember a one-day match against Australia at Bristol in 2001 when he had a problem with a finger. It was clearly in a bad way – and was later discovered to be broken – but he was still desperate to play. He actually got quite upset with me when I told him he could not play.

Then, of course, there was the famous incident on the last Ashes tour in 2002/03, when he injured his knee in the warm-up for the Adelaide Test. Physio Kirk Russell said that he was unsure whether Vaughan could play, but they went off together to the nets for a hasty fitness test. Meanwhile Nasser Hussain was waiting in his blazer ready to toss up. There was much uncertainty. Eventually Hussain decided that he could delay no longer. He had to go and toss. Luckily, as he was leaving the dressing room to do so, Vaughan returned with Russell. The problem was that

Vaughan was adamant that he wanted to play, and Russell was saying that he did not think that he should. You could not blame Russell: physios often have to err on the side of caution in such matters. But we decided to go with Vaughan's brave assertion that he was fit.

However, there were then some worried faces around when we won the toss and batted. Every run Vaughan made was watched nervously. Mind you, if we were that worried, we would have been nervous wrecks by the end of the day, because he scored a superlative 177. And he fractured a bone in his shoulder when hit by a ball from Jason Gillespie during that knock. I told you that he was tough. Funnily enough, this might have been the origin of Australia's misplaced dissatisfaction with substitutes. There was a fuss because Vaughan did not field after his epic knock. The Australians thought that he was shielding his knee, an injury which had been sustained before the game and therefore would not have warranted a substitute. But it was his shoulder which was the problem. He could barely move it. In fact we were concerned that we might have to send him home. The Australians did not believe what we were saying then. Just as they did not in this summer of 2005.

But Vaughan was not the only England batsman working very hard in the nets in between Tests. They all were, but Andrew Strauss in particular was working on a specific problem. It was plain to me that he was attempting to play spin bowling in the wrong manner. In fact I was quite surprised that no one had advised him of this before. I had spoken to him before the First Test and said that I was concerned about his preferred method.

He replied, 'Look, I'm quite comfortable with the way that I am playing, so I am going to stick with it for now.'

'That's fine,' I responded, because I never want to force anything on a player, 'but just be aware that it could get you into trouble against the very top spinners.'

Crucially, Strauss had not faced any of those before in Test cricket. We talked about this, but that was all it was – talk. I wondered whether the actual physical experience of facing Warne might change his mind. It did. After the Lord's Test he now knew that he had to change. But doing so is not that easy, especially when you have been doing something in a certain way for so long. Basically, what he was doing was playing with the spin, but using his whole body rather than just his hands to do that. So to Warne he was getting so far across his stumps that he was outside the line of the ball, something which you should never do, even when the ball is turning into you. By doing so you are letting your technique limit you to one area. Say if the ball is short and turns, then you can only hit it in the direction of fine leg – that position we term as the 45 (degrees).

Let me explain. Batting has much in common with geometry. 'Angles, angles,' I keep reminding the players in order to align themselves to hit the ball back where it comes from. That is often a fairly simple philosophy to follow, but it can become more complex, especially when facing someone like Warne. Before dealing with him, I will give you another example. Say for a moment that you are the left-handed Graham Thorpe facing Muttiah Muralitharan, as he was in Sri Lanka in 2001. The spinner will mostly bowl over the wicket, because that is what he prefers.

Apologies for a further digression, but that brings me on to an important point which I have to get off my chest briefly. Why is it that Muralitharan, and all the other sub-continent off-spinners, are allowed to bowl over the wicket at left handers without censure from the cricket-following media, while when Ashley Giles bowls his left arm spin over the wicket to right handers, he is berated wildly? There is no difference between the angles, with both looking to bowl a leg-stump line, and Muralitharan obviously turns the ball much more than Giles, so he should be the one going around the wicket! Giles has a very crossed natural action – in other words his right leg goes across his body, closing him off – making it difficult for him to bowl close to the wicket and be effective when bowling around the wicket. If he did so, he would need to turn the ball very sharply indeed to negate the angle caused by his action. That is why we have asked Giles to bowl over the wicket because then his arm is almost coming from over the stumps, bowling 'wicket-to-wicket' as the saying goes. The angle from which he is bowling also helps him in his quest to turn the ball away from the right-handed batsman.

Anyway, back to Thorpe versus Muralitharan. Thorpe's initial theory, based on what he had always been taught, was that he needed to close himself off in his stance and look to hit the ball through the off-side, even though, as we said, Muralitharan was pitching the ball on or outside the leg stump. I told him to think about how he could hit the ball back where it spins from, hitting a straight ball with a straight bat. The answer was to take guard on middle and off, and open up his stance and generally hit the ball to the leg side with a straight bat. That might seem like hitting against the spin, but the laws of geometry will back me up to prove that he was, in fact, playing a straight ball.

Remarkably, Thorpe then got himself in a tizz against the innocuous off-spin of Graeme Smith in South Africa in 2004/05. It got so bad that Smith would bring himself on to bowl almost as soon as Thorpe reached the wicket. He was all at sea because he was getting confused about his angles. He was trying to play Smith like he was Muralitharan, but there was clearly a huge difference. For one thing Smith was bowling around the wicket. For another he was pitching on off stump. And, of course, he was not turning it half as much either. Now was Thorpe's opportunity to play the ball on the off side as he had previously been advised. He could also now close his stance because by opening it there was a good chance that he could play across the line and be lbw.

I have had some fun and games with some of the England cricketers while trying to explain the laws of geometry. Because of that I actually think that it is a subject which should be taught at the National Cricket Centre at Loughborough. That way I might not have to spend so many long hours with some players.

I remember once being in Sri Lanka with Trescothick. We had a long discussion about angles. This is not to denigrate him or indeed expose him as the worst offender, because he is palpably not. Rather it is a playful aside about a cricketer I respect thoroughly. He is such a keen student of the game, always willing and eager to learn, that he was fascinated with what I was saying. But it was clearly not a subject with which he was fully *au fait*. Eventually I had to say to him, 'Tres, did you do geometry in school?'

'Not really,' he replied. So I explained everything thoroughly. I think he grasped it. But, with a day off the next day, this was too good an opportunity to miss, so I made my way into Colombo and found a stationery shop. There I bought a couple of protractors, which I took great delight in slipping under the door of his room, just in case he had not fully understood my geometry lecture. I think he saw the funny side. When I bumped into him the next day, he did not say a word, just giggled and shook his head. Mind you, that is quite usual for him. But I think his batting in recent years has proved that he might now know his angles.

I have digressed. Back to Edgbaston. So when Strauss was facing Warne he needed to stay inside the line and if the ball was pitched short enough (the length is obviously crucial because if it is fuller then you must use your hands to play with the spin) then play with a straight bat through cover, hitting the spinning ball back where it came from. Warne normally leaves a gap there too. And if the ball turned, Strauss could use his hands to hit anywhere on the leg-side, not just behind square as he was limited to beforehand.

Luckily we had a new machine which was ideal for practising such things: the much-publicised Merlin, invented by the father of *The Times* sports journalist, Matthew Pryor. Troy Cooley had been the first to mention it to me at the start of the summer. I was interested, but I obviously wanted to know how well it worked. So I asked Michael Vaughan if he fancied popping down to Loughborough to try it out. He, too, was intrigued by the idea, so after the one-day series, he went to give it a go. He liked what he saw. We both agreed that we had to get Merlin to Lord's for the First Test.

Unfortunately on its first appearance it did not work properly. It could not be used outside in the sun because the lights, which indicate when the ball is to be 'bowled', could not be seen in the glare. A number of the players were a bit sceptical at this stage. But once we took it inside and showed what it could be used for, they became more amenable. It was not long before they were admitting that they had been wrong. What we wanted to use it for was to practise dealing with Warne when he went around the wicket and pitched the ball in the rough of the bowlers' footmarks. It might seem easy to just pad the ball away, but it is not. You have got to come up with a method: do you stay back on your stumps or thrust your front leg at the ball? If you do the latter, you have got to be sure of where your stumps are. Damien Martyn found himself in trouble at Old Trafford later in the series when he was doing that to Ashley Giles, losing his off stump when Giles produced a beauty which turned from outside leg.

You have to train the brain so that when you are out there in a Test match in front of 25,000 people, you are not thinking: 'What have I got to do here?' Strauss – along with Ian Bell too – worked exceptionally hard at Edgbaston on such techniques. Matthew Maynard arrived early to help them do so. I briefed him on my chats with Strauss and he agreed with what I was saying. It is fortunate that Strauss is one of those individuals who picks up things so quickly, both mentally and technically. I have seen it before in characters like Vaughan, Trescothick and other England players who can put changes into practice almost immediately. Some other individuals you work with can strive for hours and not be able to grasp a new concept. That is what marks the difference between the top players and those ever destined to be of a standard just below.

Unfortunately Strauss made two errors in this Edgbaston Test match, which betrayed the fact that he was learning a new method. For so long his reflexes had been trained to behave in a certain manner, so that was not that surprising. There is also the awkward situation of the batsman having to think of other parts of his technique, not just this new facet. That can also lead to problems. This actually might have happened in the final Test at The Oval, where Trescothick and Strauss had been working on playing Warne with their bats in front of their pads. It is to their immense credit that they were still working at new methods that late in the series; one in which they had both done so well, too. But Trescothick might have been concentrating a little too much on Warne's good length deliveries, so that when he bowled one a bit shorter, he edged to slip, caught in two minds.

By then Strauss had in general to come to terms with his new method, quite spectacularly demonstrating that by adding a second century to his earlier effort at Old Trafford, but here at Edgbaston in the first innings he went across his stumps and tried to pad Warne away and was bowled behind his legs. OK, the ball turned extravagantly, but Strauss admitted afterwards that if he had done as we had practised, he would have been fine. And then in the second innings he attempted to cut Warne and got bowled again; he would have been better served playing that with a straight bat as we discussed above.

Merlin was a rare example of an innovation we were using becoming public knowledge. And it was not because Pryor was helping operate it – I had no problem with him helping out at the nets, because that was the only place I saw him. He was not 'in the camp' as such. Over the last few years we have not actively marketed ourselves. That is what the Australians have done. We were always hearing about their new techniques, their elaborate training camps; they were always doing this and that, and then telling the world about it. We were happy to keep our heads down and get on with the job. I have always believed that you win more games in the dressing room than outside, so we were happy to keep most of what we were doing in there to ourselves.

I will give you an example of something we did recently which was kept quiet. It was not earth-shatteringly important – that is why I am telling you now – but I think that it illustrates what I am saying.

You might have heard of Sherylle Calder, once a South African hockey player, who is now a renowned vision specialist. She is probably best known for having worked with the England rugby squad before their World Cup triumph of 2003. She has also worked with, among others, the Australian cricket squad and the All Blacks rugby squad. But she also worked with the England cricket squad during last winter's South Africa tour.

We did not publicise this because I have never believed in boasting about such things. But I had actually first used her specialist knowledge when I was at Western Province in 1996 and arranged for her to do some work with the players there. She even helped my son, Michael, with an eye problem. He was having problems studying, unable to read properly, which really worried me, so I asked Calder to take a look at him. She asked him: 'Have you got a computer?'

'Yes,' he replied.

'Where is it?' she asked. It so happened that the computer was positioned to one side of his desk, and consequently one of his eyes was getting lazy. She prescribed him a set of eye exercises – and moved his computer to facing him straight on – which cured the problem within a couple of weeks.

She did some eye-training exercises with the Western Province team which were such hard work for the players' eyes that when we attempted a fielding session soon afterwards, they could not catch a thing. In fact I had to abandon the practice. It proved what Calder had been telling us; that cricketers do not use their eye muscles enough to train their eyes. That is why using a vision coach like her can be invaluable.

We did not push things that far with the England squad but Calder did conduct some basic tests with them. We never force players in these instances if they are not receptive, but a few players did decide that it was best for them to pursue some further work in this field. It might have helped this summer. It might not.

Apologies for more digression, but back to Edgbaston again. I do not know how much Australia have used a vision coach, but no matter how hard someone like Calder could have worked with Glenn McGrath, she could never have trained his eyes sufficiently to have seen a cricket ball lying behind him. Eyes in the back of your head, and all that. Because it was here that McGrath trod and damaged his ankle on such a ball on the first morning of the Test. I cannot deny that his withdrawal from the match gave us an enormous lift. How could it not? He had taken 9 for 82 in the match at Lord's, and is one of the great fast bowlers of all time.

But. Yes, there is a corollary. As I said, at Lord's everything was in his favour. Previous to that I had seen signs that he was on the wane a little. We had never hit him around with such ease at the death in one-day matches before, for instance. It seemed to me that unless the ball was seaming about, he would not find wickets so easy to come by at this advanced stage of his career. I think that he would have struggled at Edgbaston.

We will never know. What we did know at ten o'clock on that first morning was that we were batting. I do not usually watch the toss taking place, so while I was pottering around the dressing room, I heard the shout go up that we were batting. I thought to myself: 'Great toss to win, Vaughany.' It was then that I was informed that Ricky Ponting had won the toss and inserted us. To say that it was a surprise would be to understate my reaction. It was a complete shock. What was he thinking? There had been no doubt in our minds that we were going to bat. He must have been duped by all that talk of a damp pitch; he must have thought that there was some moisture in it. There was not. Yes, there was a possibility that it might seam around a little in the first hour, but that is the case with most Test pitches. Maybe he should have changed tack once McGrath went down, but that would not have shown faith in his replacement Mike

Kasprowicz. I didn't really care. That was their problem. I was just very happy that we were batting.

We got off to a flyer. You normally say that about an opening partnership in a one-day match, but this was Test cricket at its most exhilarating. Trescothick and Strauss put on 112 in quick time to set an inspirational tone and tempo, as we scored at over five runs an over throughout the day. The words about increased positivity with the bat manifested themselves in some wonderful strokeplay. No longer were we just waiting for the bad ball as we had been at Lord's, even though there were plenty of those bowled up front as the Australians hit bad lengths. It does take two to tango. It is fine looking to be positive, but if you score at the rate which we were for such a long period, then the bowlers must be doing something wrong as well.

Trescothick scored 90, his highest score against Australia in Tests, which really delighted me because it vindicated my decision to allow him to play in the Twenty20 Finals day. As I said earlier, it was my hope that it would free him up mentally and take him away from the worries about his technique, even though it was in a pressurised atmosphere. If he had batted in a four-day game he would have used it as a practice session and probably complicated matters further. That was my thinking.

As it was for Andrew Flintoff. He had looked a little tense at Lord's – maybe trying too hard in his first Ashes Test – but here he expressed himself magnificently. It was just a case of saying to him, 'Listen, just go out there – be positive. Don't make the game too complicated – just stick to the basics.' Five sixes and six fours in a rapid 68 off 62 balls suggest that there was not too much cluttering his mind! It was here that his glorious summer really began, although we should not forget that in a fairly nondescript (for him, anyway) performance at Lord's he did dismiss Adam Gilchrist twice. That was to prove seminal.

To add to a second-innings 73, his bowling throughout the match was quite extraordinary, especially in their second innings where his spell of 3 for 23 rocked their top order. The first over he bowled in that innings will live long in the memory: its first ball bowling Justin Langer and it was no surprise when Ponting edged behind to Geraint Jones off the last, because the Australian skipper had found terror in every ball he faced. It was ferocious stuff.

It was in this match that it began to become clear that the Australians were going to struggle with reverse swing in this series. Both Flintoff and Simon Jones can reverse-swing the ball both ways, which is unusual because most bowlers can only produce the late swing into the right-handed batsman with the old ball. It was immediately obvious that the Australians did not like this. And what is more, the reverse swing was beginning to occur early in the innings too. That was due to our keeping the ball very dry. There are various theories about how best to produce reverse swing. A few senior England bowlers in the past have insisted that it is easiest achieved by wetting one side of the ball. Remember that as coach I can only consult; the players have to take responsibility for the decisions which they make. But I had spoken to Waqar Younis at Glamorgan in 1997 and he had confirmed that he liked to keep the whole ball very dry. That means the fielders have to be very careful not to clasp the ball with sweaty palms; just use two fingers to hold it by the seam. You can shine one side, but the other side must remain as dry as a bone. It seemed to be working.

Flintoff and Kevin Pietersen put on 103 for the fifth wicket in the first innings; Pietersen's 71 being a third successive fifty. The pity was that, as at Lord's in both innings, no one really stayed with him. It is difficult for a batsman in those circumstances, juggling individual and team priorities. He deserved a hundred in at least one of those three innings, because they were all high-quality efforts. But that maiden century could wait for another day. A very important day.

Michael Vaughan only scored 24 in the first innings here but I thought he looked very good. He was bowled cheaply again in the second innings but I thought he had turned a corner. As had his pal Ashley Giles, who responded to all that ridiculous criticism beforehand with a gutsy performance with the ball, as we dismissed the Australians for 308 first time around. That lead of 99 proved crucial, because we laboured in our second innings, only Flintoff excelling. That left Australia 282 to win and when they were 175–8 at close of play on Saturday evening (after Steve Harmison had snared Michael Clarke with a stunning slower ball with the last ball of the day), still needing 107 for victory, everyone was saying that it was already our game.

I wasn't saying that. International cricket is not like that any more. The days of numbers nine, ten and eleven just wandering out to the middle and having a quick slog are gone. It is a mindset I have had to alter among some of the England players, implanted from county cricket no doubt – although that is changing.

So we knew that it was not all over when we began play on that Sunday morning. Brett Lee, first with Warne and then with Kasprowicz, took Australia to within two runs of victory in an agonisingly tense session of play. Then Kasprowicz gloved a short ball from Harmison to be caught by Geraint Jones diving forward to cue wild celebrations. The series was back to 1–1. Vaughan said afterwards that it would have been difficult to have come back from 2–0 down against a side as good as Australia. He was right.

I might not show too much emotion, but I was churning inside that morning. There was a very close lbw decision on Kasprowicz early on in his innings when moving across his stumps. That decision could have cost us dear. I do not generally complain about umpiring decisions, but when they are concerning the last wicket, they can obviously become vital. OK, Australia can complain that they had Simon Jones lbw the previous day, before he helped put on a crucial 51 runs for the last wicket. But no matter, it turned out rosy for us in the end, meaning that a DVD was made soon afterwards proclaiming it to be 'The Greatest Test'. Little did they know what was going to follow.

## Second Test
*England v. Australia*
*Edgbaston, Birmingham*
*4–7 August 2005*

**Umpires:** B. Bowden (NZ) and R. Koertzen (SA)
**Toss:** Australia

| England: 1st innings | | | R | M | B | 4 | 6 |
|---|---|---|---|---|---|---|---|
| M. Trescothick | c Gilchrist | b Kasprowicz | 90 | 143 | 102 | 15 | 2 |
| A. Strauss | | b Warne | 48 | 113 | 76 | 10 | 0 |
| *M. Vaughan | c Lee | b Gillespie | 24 | 54 | 41 | 3 | 0 |
| I. Bell | c Gilchrist | b Kasprowicz | 6 | 2 | 3 | 1 | 0 |
| K. Pietersen | c Katich | b Lee | 71 | 152 | 76 | 10 | 1 |
| A. Flintoff | c Gilchrist | b Gillespie | 68 | 74 | 62 | 6 | 5 |
| +G. Jones | c Gilchrist | b Kasprowicz | 1 | 14 | 15 | 0 | 0 |
| A. Giles | lbw | b Warne | 23 | 34 | 30 | 4 | 0 |
| M. Hoggard | lbw | b Warne | 16 | 62 | 49 | 2 | 0 |
| S. Harmison | | b Warne | 17 | 16 | 11 | 2 | 1 |
| S. Jones | not out | | 19 | 39 | 24 | 1 | 1 |
| Extras | (lb 9, w 1, nb 14) | | 24 | | | | |
| Total | (all out, 79.2 overs, 356 mins) | | 407 | | | | |

FoW: 1–112 (Strauss, 25.3 ov), 2–164 (Trescothick, 32.3 ov), 3–170 (Bell, 32.6 ov), 4–187 (Vaughan, 36.6 ov), 5–290 (Flintoff, 54.3 ov), 6–293 (G. Jones, 57.4 ov), 7–342 (Giles, 65.1 ov), 8–348 (Pietersen, 66.3 ov), 9–375 (Harmison, 69.4 ov), 10–407 (Hoggard, 79.2 ov).

| Bowling | O | M | R | W |
|---|---|---|---|---|
| Lee | 17 | 1 | 111 | 1 |
| Gillespie | 22 | 3 | 91 | 2 |
| Kasprowicz | 15 | 3 | 80 | 3 |
| Warne | 25.2 | 4 | 116 | 4 |

| Australia: 1st innings | | | R | M | B | 4 | 6 |
|---|---|---|---|---|---|---|---|
| J. Langer | lbw | b S. Jones | 82 | 276 | 154 | 7 | 0 |
| M. Hayden | c Strauss | b Hoggard | 0 | 5 | 1 | 0 | 0 |
| *R. Ponting | c Vaughan | b Giles | 61 | 87 | 76 | 12 | 0 |
| D. Martyn | run out (Vaughan) | | 20 | 23 | 18 | 4 | 0 |
| M. Clarke | c G. Jones | b Giles | 40 | 85 | 68 | 7 | 0 |
| S. Katich | c G. Jones | b Flintoff | 4 | 22 | 18 | 1 | 0 |
| +A. Gilchrist | not out | | 49 | 120 | 69 | 4 | 0 |
| S. Warne | | b Giles | 8 | 14 | 14 | 2 | 0 |
| B. Lee | c Flintoff | b S. Jones | 6 | 14 | 10 | 1 | 0 |
| J. Gillespie | lbw | b Flintoff | 7 | 36 | 37 | 1 | 0 |
| M. Kasprowicz | lbw | b Flintoff | 0 | 1 | 1 | 0 | 0 |
| Extras | (b 13, lb 7, w 1, nb 10) | | 31 | | | | |
| Total | (all out, 76 overs, 346 mins) | | 308 | | | | |

FoW: 1–0 (Hayden, 1.1 ov), 2–88 (Ponting, 19.5 ov), 3–118 (Martyn, 24.5 ov), 4–194 (Clarke, 44.2 ov), 5–208 (Katich, 49.4 ov), 6–262 (Langer, 61.3 ov), 7–273 (Warne, 64.5 ov), 8–282 (Lee, 67.1 ov), 9–308 (Gillespie, 75.5 ov), 10–308 (Kasprowicz, 75.6 ov).

| Bowling | O | M | R | W |
|---|---|---|---|---|
| Harmison | 11 | 1 | 48 | 0 |
| Hoggard | 8 | 0 | 41 | 1 |
| S. Jones | 16 | 2 | 69 | 2 |
| Flintoff | 15 | 1 | 52 | 3 |
| Giles | 26 | 2 | 78 | 3 |

| England: 2nd innings | | | R | M | B | 4 | 6 |
|---|---|---|---|---|---|---|---|
| M. Trescothick | c Gilchrist | b Lee | 21 | 51 | 38 | 4 | 0 |
| A. Strauss | | b Warne | 6 | 28 | 12 | 1 | 0 |
| M. Hoggard | c Hayden | b Lee | 1 | 35 | 27 | 0 | 0 |
| *M. Vaughan | | b Lee | 1 | 2 | 2 | 0 | 0 |
| I. Bell | c Gilchrist | b Warne | 21 | 69 | 43 | 2 | 0 |
| K. Pietersen | c Gilchrist | b Warne | 20 | 50 | 35 | 0 | 2 |
| A. Flintoff | | b Warne | 73 | 133 | 86 | 6 | 4 |
| +G. Jones | c Ponting | b Lee | 9 | 33 | 19 | 1 | 0 |
| A. Giles | c Hayden | b Warne | 8 | 44 | 36 | 0 | 0 |
| S. Harmison | c Ponting | b Warne | 0 | 2 | 1 | 0 | 0 |
| S. Jones | not out | | 12 | 42 | 23 | 3 | 0 |
| Extras | (lb 1, nb 9) | | 10 | | | | |
| Total | (all out, 52.1 overs, 249 mins) | | 182 | | | | |

FoW: 1–25 (Strauss, 6.2 ov), 2–27 (Trescothick, 11.2 ov), 3–29 (Vaughan, 11.5 ov), 4–31 (Hoggard, 13.5 ov), 5–72 (Pietersen, 24.6 ov), 6–75 (Bell, 26.5 ov), 7–101 (G. Jones, 33.6 ov), 8–131 (Giles, 44.3 ov), 9–131 (Harmison, 44.4 ov), 10–182 (Flintoff, 52.1 ov).

| Bowling | O | M | R | W |
|---|---|---|---|---|
| Lee | 18 | 1 | 82 | 4 |
| Gillespie | 8 | 0 | 24 | 0 |
| Kasprowicz | 3 | 0 | 29 | 0 |
| Warne | 23.1 | 7 | 46 | 6 |

| *Australia: 2nd innings (Target: 282 runs)* | | | *R* | *M* | *B* | *4* | *6* |
|---|---|---|---|---|---|---|---|
| J. Langer | | b Flintoff | 28 | 54 | 47 | 4 | 0 |
| M. Hayden | c Trescothick | b S. Jones | 31 | 106 | 64 | 4 | 0 |
| *R. Ponting | c G. Jones | b Flintoff | 0 | 4 | 5 | 0 | 0 |
| D. Martyn | c Bell | b Hoggard | 28 | 64 | 36 | 5 | 0 |
| M. Clarke | | b Harmison | 30 | 101 | 57 | 4 | 0 |
| S. Katich | c Trescothick | b Giles | 16 | 27 | 21 | 3 | 0 |
| +A. Gilchrist | c Flintoff | b Giles | 1 | 8 | 4 | 0 | 0 |
| J. Gillespie | lbw | b Flintoff | 0 | 4 | 2 | 0 | 0 |
| S. Warne | hit wicket | b Flintoff | 42 | 79 | 59 | 4 | 2 |
| B. Lee | not out | | 43 | 99 | 75 | 5 | 0 |
| M. Kasprowicz | c G. Jones | b Harmison | 20 | 60 | 31 | 3 | 0 |
| Extras | (b 13, lb 8, w 1, nb 18) | | 40 | | | | |
| Total | (all out, 64.3 overs, 307 mins) | | 279 | | | | |

FoW: 1–47 (Langer, 12.2 ov), 2–48 (Ponting, 12.6 ov), 3–82 (Hayden, 22.5 ov), 4–107 (Martyn, 26.1 ov), 5–134 (Katich, 31.6 ov), 6–136 (Gilchrist, 33.5 ov), 7–137 (Gillespie, 34.2 ov), 8–175 (Clarke, 43.4 ov), 9–220 (Warne, 52.1 ov), 10–279 (Kasprowicz, 64.3 ov).

| *Bowling* | *O* | *M* | *R* | *W* |
|---|---|---|---|---|
| Harmison | 17.3 | 3 | 62 | 2 |
| Hoggard | 5 | 0 | 26 | 1 |
| Giles | 15 | 3 | 68 | 2 |
| Flintoff | 22 | 3 | 79 | 4 |
| S. Jones | 5 | 1 | 23 | 1 |

**Result:** England won by 2 runs
**Man of the Match:** A. Flintoff
**Series:** Level at 1–1

# 5

Thank goodness that the Edgbaston Test finished on the Sunday. It gave both sides an extra day off before the next encounter at Old Trafford. Three days off instead of two then. Not exactly complete recuperation.

This was gruelling stuff, but back-to-back Test matches are not unusual in international cricket these days. Not that it necessarily makes them any easier. So fatigue was an issue even before this Test started. Please remember that; it might come in handy later in the chapter. You will see why.

It was a good toss for Michael Vaughan to win. It was obvious that it was a bat-first pitch. There had been a lot of talk beforehand about the possible make-up of the Australian attack; Brett Lee had been in hospital with an infected knee and Glenn McGrath suddenly appeared to bowl at a net session. It was almost as if we were playing an England side of years ago. We could not concern ourselves with that, though. Whomever we were going to be facing, we had to be positive, just like Edgbaston.

As it was, they both played. And we played positively again. By the end of day one we were 341–5. Edgbaston had been exciting, but I was not sure that you could play like that too often and get away with it. This was more controlled in its construction. And the funny thing is that the outfield was so slow that I think we could easily have added at least forty runs to this total on a Birmingham outfield. So maybe this was an even more pleasing start than there.

It certainly was for the captain, who hit the first hundred of the series. I knew that he had been batting well. And he had said so in public himself, so it would have been gratifying for him to have proved that he could walk the walk, as well as talk the talk. He did give a couple of early chances, but which batsman doesn't at some stage? Thereafter he played magnificently. It was typical of him that once he went past 50 he should go on to make a big hundred. That is what he does. He is very, very good at making it count.

Talking of counting, I must mention Shane Warne's achievement of reaching 600 Test wickets. I've already mentioned the word 'great' in reference to him and it is not wasted on him. He truly is a champion of the sport; a bowler of the highest quality with a very good cricketing brain to match. It is interesting to note how different the performances of Australia have been when he has been absent. For example when India travelled to Australia in 2003/04 and drew the series, neither Warne nor McGrath was playing. When Warne retires, I do not think that Australia will be anywhere near as competitive as they are now on the Test scene.

Mind you, I do have to say that he was very lucky to get his 600th in the manner in which he did here. Marcus Trescothick was playing well when he swept at him. He had gone through with the shot when it hit the back of his bat; the ball then struck Gilchrist on the knee, bounced up on to his chin and then finally into his gloves! What was I saying about luck, though? Well done to Warne.

Ian Bell came good in this game as well, making two nice fifties. He had to really fight at some stages and he came through them well, I thought. We really do like to be consistent with our selections and Bell is a case in point. Even after that First Test some people were calling for his head. It's ridiculous. Why do they want to write players off so quickly? It's like they are kids and becoming bored of their new toy; they want to maintain interest by bringing someone new in.

It was the same with Ashley Giles before he answered his critics at Edgbaston. It is no coincidence that the two players who receive most criticism in our side are the spinner and the wicketkeeper. There is only ever one wicketkeeper in a side and often only one spinner, so their performances are highlighted more than others. If you are a member of a four-pronged seam attack, and you bowl badly, you are given a rest and someone else does your job. Your poor performance is easily forgotten. The same applies to a batsman when there might be at least five others to do the job. The poor spinner and wicketkeeper, they are one of a kind and if they perform badly, they receive both barrels. Giles bowled very well again here, taking three wickets on the second day so that Australia were 214–7 at the close on Friday, still 31 runs short of avoiding the follow-on. Not that that mattered. For one, we were never going to enforce that here, and for two, they ended up making 302 all out. Just like I was saying, Geraint Jones missed a couple of chances on the rain-blighted Saturday and he was lambasted.

For the other Jones, Simon, there was nothing but joy unconfined, as he claimed Test best figures of 6–53 in the first innings. His coming of age this summer was one of the key factors in this series. The potential has always been there. It was a long time ago that I identified him and Steve Harmison as being fast bowlers who might play for England. When a provisional list for the National Academy intake for Australia in 2001/02 was handed to me, somewhat blithely I said, 'I don't care who goes as long as Jones and Harmison do.' I clearly did not intend for that to be taken literally, but you get my drift.

Against New Zealand at Lord's in 2004 we saw what Simon Jones could really do in international cricket. There was a spell of reverse swing there which opened a lot of people's eyes. Or it should have done. When he began reverse-swinging the ball both ways this summer, it was said that he had never done that before. Only into the right-hander, they said. Wrong. He had shown that he could reverse-swing it both ways that day at Lord's.

Troy Cooley has done wonders with all the bowlers, but now and again I do speak to some of them. And that had been the case last winter when I spoke to Jones during the one-day trip to Namibia and Zimbabwe. I mentioned about his grip on the ball. His first two fingers were close together down a straight seam. Instead I wanted him to open those fingers out a little with the seam slightly tilted towards first and second slip. He immediately announced that his wrist felt stronger behind the ball. And that winter he began to bowl a conventional out-swinger regularly. His accuracy also improved markedly. Interestingly, even though he did so well in this Test at Old Trafford I did pick up that in the second innings he was reverting to old habits. The seam was straightening again and the fingers getting closer together. I mentioned this to him, and he did not believe me. Luckily, of course, we have instant proof on hand. A quick look at the computer screens manned by analyst Tim Boon, using his E-Cricket (now called Feedback Analysis) equipment, and all was revealed.

This is not to say that I am claiming sole credit for Jones's advances. I cannot hand Cooley enough praise for his role with the bowlers. They all have enormous respect for him as a mentor and a coach; psychologically he fits into their group superbly and I feel that I can work closely with him in a relationship of trust and mutual respect. England have the best four-pronged seam attack in the world at the moment; Cooley must take much credit for that. As in this example with Jones here, sometimes I will help one of the bowlers, but it is also just as likely that he will help one of the batsmen. In fact I encourage all of the off-field management team to help with the coaching in some way – Matthew Maynard obviously, but also Boon and Phil Neale too. If any of these has spotted something with a player, they will bounce it off me first, because we do not want any contradictory advice going to the player. I do like the fact that not everyone has to stick rigidly to their job description.

I must admit that I was surprised how poorly the Australian batsmen dealt with reverse swing in this series; all these so-called world-class batsmen coming over here to be suddenly befuddled by it. More surprising was how open they were in their admission of a problem with it. They must have known that Jones and Flintoff would be able to produce it. Jones has a skiddy, slingy-type action which lends itself naturally to reverse swing and, as I said, has shown previously what he can do. Flintoff's action does not immediately strike one as being tailor-made for reverse swing but he does fall away a little which helps him to achieve it. The bowler whose action I would never think suitable for reverse swing is McGrath. He is so upright and classical that it was a real surprise how effective he was at producing it.

In fairness to the Australians Flintoff had never really shown that he could swing the ball away in reverse fashion before this series. I think that really caught them on the hop. The manner in which he set up Simon Katich in the first innings here at Manchester was outstanding: bowling around the wicket and taking the ball away from him before darting one back into him as the left hander shouldered arms. That was very clever.

As was Jones's dismissal of Michael Clarke in the second innings. He, too, left a ball, only to be bowled. These were not batsmen who knew which way the ball was swinging. There was a great deal of uncertainty. Which was something which seemed to have disappeared from Andrew Strauss's mind when he was making a first Ashes century in the second innings. All that work with Merlin had paid off so that he could deal with Warne, who had been making some comments about Strauss's weaknesses against him. We'd identified the problem and worked it out. That is always satisfying. Strauss showed some courage too, because Lee hit him on the ear, drawing blood, so that when he took off his helmet to celebrate his hundred he rather comically revealed a bit of sticky plaster on his ear.

Bell made that second half-century of the match but there was also a brilliant little cameo from Geraint Jones, who made 27 not out from just 12 balls, with two sixes. McGrath finished with five wickets but never before can he have done so in such a fashion in a Test match, with fielders scattered around the boundary and batsmen prepared to sacrifice their wickets in the quest for quick runs. It all meant that we could declare to leave Australia 423 to win. Some people pointed out at the time that that is what Australia used to do to England, but I did not look at it in that way. England should do what England do well; which they have been doing for the last two years. We should not want to copy anyone. We should do it our way and then let others copy us.

The final day at Old Trafford was incredible. They tell me that 20,000 people were turned away at the gates. It seemed like more. It was chaos. I normally like to get to the ground early, at about 8 a.m., but even at that time there was gridlock. I feared that I might be late for the warm-up at 9.15. My wife, Marina, came to the ground in a taxi with some players' wives just after play had begun, and she thought that there might have been a bomb-scare. It seemed to her like a mass evacuation as there were so many people walking away from the ground.

It was heartening for us to see how much interest there was in this series, even if this was only the Third Test. It is the first time that I can recall our running through a warm-up to a fully packed ground. Normally there are swathes of open spaces with spectators still coming into the ground, but this was different. It definitely put an extra spring in the players' strides.

Those fans who made it into the ground could have asked for little more in terms of entertainment. One more wicket, I suppose, for the win. But we gave it everything on a pitch which did not deteriorate as much as we expected, or indeed hoped. It became very slow and it was easy enough for the batsmen to adjust when the ball did do anything. Ricky Ponting played very well for his hundred, but I could not help feeling that the Australians had been fortunate. Even when he had passed his century he still played and missed regularly with the ball not finding the edge. We were also handicapped by an ill-timed bout of cramp which affected Simon Jones with seven overs remaining. That was a huge loss. His substitute Stephen Peters might have run out Brett Lee just after too. Some have questioned whether we should have taken the new ball in the 81st over because the old one seemed to be reverse-swinging nicely at that stage. But it was the correct decision. There were another 27 overs bowled in the day. It gave us an opportunity to use conventional swing with the new one and enough time for the ball to start reversing as well. If it had not rained so much on the Saturday we would surely have won the match. There was not a session which Australia could be said to have dominated here. We deserved to be 2–1 up.

There were other matters concerning me on that final Monday. The semi-finals of the Cheltenham & Gloucester Trophy were to take place on the following Saturday. They were between Warwickshire and Lancashire at Edgbaston, and Hampshire and Yorkshire at Southampton. Six players on duty at Old Trafford might be expected to feature in these matches: Bell and Giles for Warwickshire; Flintoff for Lancashire; Pietersen for Hampshire; and Vaughan and Matthew Hoggard for Yorkshire.

Normally it would have been a no-brainer. None of them would have been allowed to play. Please recall what I said at the top of this chapter. The players were tired before this Test. Now they had played in two of the most intense, exhausting – physically and mentally – back-to-back Test matches that anyone could possibly imagine. They were shattered. But this was slightly different in that there is a special contractual agreement between the ECB and C&G that centrally contracted players must be released to play in the C&G Trophy.

Usually during a Test Phil Neale will come to me with a spreadsheet, detailing what county cricket there is coming up. I will analyse it, looking at where players might be playing, how much travelling they might be doing, while always bearing in mind how tired the players might be. And remember that I consider mental tiredness to be more of a concern than physical fatigue. We have got a saying which I keep reiterating to the team: 'Tiredness is in the brain.' That keeps players going during Test matches.

By the Sunday we already had three injury concerns. Vaughan had been off the field a number of times because of soreness to his troublesome knee. He was very worried about it and had got physio Kirk Russell to check it a few times. Flintoff's ankle was troubling him; the same one which had been operated upon before the summer began. So he had come off the field a few times just to receive reassurance from Russell that it was not a recurrence of the initial problem. But the biggest worry was over Giles's hip, which seemed to be flaring up again. I spoke to Russell about them and said that we definitely needed to rest these three. Their county physios were then informed and Peter Gregory, the ECB's chief medical officer, was called to come in and see the players on Monday morning. The decision was then out of my hands, but those three were immediately pulled out of the semi-finals. Either the chairman or the chief executive of each county, as well as John Carr, ECB's director of cricket operations, was then informed.

I receive an awful amount of stick for not communicating with the counties about these issues, but it is not my job to do that. That is Phil Neale's job. As with any decision-making process I always think that there should only be one point of reference – that is Neale. I cannot be making a mountain of phone calls during a Test match. In fact I am not allowed to. Since the betting scandals reared their ugly heads, it is an ICC regulation that only the operations manager can have a phone on in the dressing room. Only he can use it too. I have got quite enough to worry about already, thank you very much. What I always say to Neale is that if there is ever a significant problem with a county, then I will make a personal call later if necessary. But only if absolutely necessary. That became the case here.

Warne takes 6 for 46 during our second innings, the best figures of the series. We
ggled to 182, setting the Australians 282 to win.

18. Flintoff has Jason Gillespie lbw for a duck, leaving Australia reeling on 137 for 7, still 145 runs short.

19. Phew! Harmison finally snares Kasprowicz, taken down the leg side by Jones. Australia are all out for 279, giving us victory by just 2 runs.

20. Vaughan and man-of-the-match Flintoff celebra the end of an extraordina and nailbiting Test match The series is level at 1–1.

Hard work rewarded. Vaughan contributes a magnificent 166 on the first day of the rd Test at Old Trafford.

22. Geraint Jones cuts Warne during his first-innings knock of 42. Gilchrist looks on.

23. Warne celebrates his record 600th Test dismissal – Trescothick caught (rather luckily!) by Gilchrist for 63 during our first-innings total of 444. The master showed he had lost none of his skill or competitive spirit, and would go on to take 40 wickets in the series, setting a new record for wickets against England by an Australian.

24. Andrew Flintoff is congratulated after bowling Simon Katich for 17.

25. Simon Jones bowled superbly well to help restrict Australia to 302 in their first innings, taking a career-best 6 for 53. Here he has the prize scalp of Adam Gilchrist, caught behind for 30.

26. Surprise package. Warne shows his skills with bat as well as ball – he scored more run in the series than Martyn, Katich and Gilchrist, and top-scored in Australia's first innings with 90.

27. Thanks Merlin. Andrew Straus acknowledges the crowd as he reac his century in our second innings; reward for many hours spent practising how to combat Shane Warne.

Ricky Ponting takes one in the ribs during his match-saving knock of 156.

29. With Warne gone, caught by Geraint Jones off Flintoff for 34, Australia were 340 for

30. But Lee and McGrath saw Australia home, with us striving in vain for the crucial final wicket. A draw left the series still in the balance, with two matches to play.

The other three players had smaller niggles. Bell had a shoulder problem which meant that he did not throw over-arm at all during that Test or indeed for the remainder of the series. Hoggard had a small knee problem and Pietersen was having problems with his elbow. That is an old injury initially suffered in a car accident when he was young, and it was affecting his throwing. When it becomes extremely sore it can affect his batting too.

I spoke to Gregory about these. He said that on purely medical grounds he could not pull them out. They could play, but they were exhausted and they ran the risk of worsening those niggles. And, of course, there was that mental fatigue to consider. What people do not appreciate is that I have to manage these processes for the players. I have to look beyond tomorrow and try to gauge the long-term effects.

The players are also placed in a very difficult position. I can fully understand the loyalty they often show to their counties. They might be tired and know that they should not play, but often they do not want their counties to know that they do not want to play.

I decided to speak to Carr. I told him that I knew that there was a contractual agreement with C&G but that I thought that it was in the best interests of English cricket if all these players were withdrawn from the semi-finals. We needed them fit and fresh when they were reporting to Trent Bridge the following week. He agreed. 'Leave it with me,' he said. He spoke to C&G and they were very supportive, so much so that I made a point of phoning them afterwards to thank them.

There was only one problem – that we knew of at this stage, anyway. Hampshire were not happy. They desperately wanted Pietersen to play. So I phoned Rod Bransgrove, their chairman. After a rather awkward start we have become good friends over time. I have a lot of respect for what he is doing at Hampshire and I think that he understands and appreciates what I am doing with England. When I explained the situation to him in some detail, he was very receptive. He agreed that it was right for Pietersen not to play. I was happy that the whole country seemed to be united in their support behind the England team.

That was until the news broke that we were going to rest these players. I should have known that there was going to be some criticism. It came from predictable sources. With it the issue was also raised of Vaughan's benefit match, a Twenty20 encounter between England and Yorkshire which was scheduled to take place on the Wednesday after the Trent Bridge Test. It was said that I would be hypocritical if I allowed the players to participate in that and not the C&G semi-finals. I totally disagreed. It was not a concern to me. I had spoken to the captain about it long before, and I had said that if players were tired, especially the bowlers, then they were not to bowl in that benefit match. But more than anything that match would be a bit of fun. It would have only lasted for three hours anyway. As I keep reiterating, most of the time I don't pull players out of cricket because I fear that they will get injured. They could just as easily do some damage to themselves on a golf course. But nobody would have complained if it had been a Michael Vaughan Benefit golf day.

With these semi-finals it would not just have been a case of 'pitch and play' for the players. They could not switch off mentally and then suddenly turn up on the Saturday. If they were being professional about it – which I'm sure they would – they would have had to start thinking about the game some forty-eight hours beforehand. They would have had to practise on the Friday before the game. They would have played the match on the Saturday and then had to report for the Test on the Monday night. Add that on to the after-effects of the back-to-back Tests and they would have been mentally shattered.

Not convinced? I have some proof. Ashley Giles wanted to play in the semi-final. In fact he was most upset when I told him that he could not. So I phoned him on the Friday. 'How are you?' I asked.

'Physically I feel fine,' he replied, 'but mentally I am still tired.' QED.

# Third Test

*England v Australia*
*Old Trafford, Manchester*
*11–15 August 2005*

**Umpires:** B. Bowden (NZ) and S. Bucknor (WI)
**Toss:** England

| *England: 1st innings* | | | R | M | B | 4 | 6 |
|---|---|---|---|---|---|---|---|
| M. Trescothick | c Gilchrist | b Warne | 63 | 196 | 117 | 9 | 0 |
| A. Strauss | | b Lee | 6 | 43 | 28 | 0 | 0 |
| *M. Vaughan | c McGrath | b Katich | 166 | 281 | 215 | 20 | 1 |
| I. Bell | c Gilchrist | b Lee | 59 | 205 | 155 | 8 | 0 |
| K. Pietersen | c sub (Hodge) | b Lee | 21 | 50 | 28 | 1 | 0 |
| M. Hoggard | | b Lee | 4 | 13 | 10 | 1 | 0 |
| A. Flintoff | c Langer | b Warne | 46 | 93 | 67 | 7 | 0 |
| +G. Jones | | b Gillespie | 42 | 86 | 51 | 6 | 0 |
| A. Giles | c Hayden | b Warne | 0 | 11 | 6 | 0 | 0 |
| S. Harmison | not out | | 10 | 13 | 11 | 1 | 0 |
| S. Jones | | b Warne | 0 | 7 | 4 | 0 | 0 |
| Extras | (b 4, lb 5, w 3, nb 15) | | 27 | | | | |
| Total | (all out, 113.2 overs, 503 mins) | | 444 | | | | |

FoW: 1–26 (Strauss, 9.2 ov), 2–163 (Trescothick, 41.5 ov), 3–290 (Vaughan, 74.3 ov), 4–333 (Pietersen, 86.2 ov), 5–341 (Hoggard, 88.6 ov), 6–346 (Bell, 92.1 ov), 7–433 (Flintoff, 109.2 ov), 8–434 (G. Jones, 110.2 ov), 9–438 (Giles, 111.4 ov), 10–444 (S. Jones, 113.2 ov).

| Bowling | O | M | R | W |
|---|---|---|---|---|
| McGrath | 25 | 6 | 86 | 0 |
| Lee | 27 | 6 | 100 | 4 |
| Gillespie | 19 | 2 | 114 | 1 |
| Warne | 33.2 | 5 | 99 | 4 |
| Katich | 9 | 1 | 36 | 1 |

| Australia: 1st innings | | | R | M | B | 4 | 6 |
|---|---|---|---|---|---|---|---|
| J. Langer | c Bell | b Giles | 31 | 76 | 50 | 4 | 0 |
| M. Hayden | lbw | b Giles | 34 | 112 | 71 | 5 | 0 |
| *R. Ponting | c Bell | b S. Jones | 7 | 20 | 12 | 1 | 0 |
| D. Martyn | | b Giles | 20 | 71 | 41 | 2 | 0 |
| S. Katich | | b Flintoff | 17 | 39 | 28 | 1 | 0 |
| +A. Gilchrist | c G. Jones | b S. Jones | 30 | 74 | 49 | 4 | 0 |
| S. Warne | c Giles | b S. Jones | 90 | 183 | 122 | 11 | 1 |
| M. Clarke | c Flintoff | b S. Jones | 7 | 19 | 18 | 0 | 0 |
| J. Gillespie | lbw | b S. Jones | 26 | 144 | 111 | 1 | 1 |
| B. Lee | c Trescothick | b S. Jones | 1 | 17 | 16 | 0 | 0 |
| G. McGrath | not out | | 1 | 20 | 4 | 0 | 0 |
| Extras | (b 8, lb 7, w 8, nb 15) | | 38 | | | | |
| Total | (all out, 84.5 overs, 393 mins) | | 302 | | | | |

FoW: 1–58 (Langer, 15.5 ov), 2–73 (Ponting, 20.1 ov), 3–86 (Hayden, 23.3 ov), 4–119 (Katich, 32.1 ov), 5–133 (Martyn, 35.3 ov), 6–186 (Gilchrist, 48.1 ov), 7–201 (Clarke, 52.3 ov), 8–287 (Warne, 76.2 ov), 9–293 (Lee, 80.4 ov), 10–302 (Gillespie, 84.5 ov).

| Bowling | O | M | R | W |
|---|---|---|---|---|
| Harmison | 10 | 0 | 47 | 0 |
| Hoggard | 6 | 2 | 22 | 0 |
| Flintoff | 20 | 1 | 65 | 1 |
| S. Jones | 17.5 | 6 | 53 | 6 |
| Giles | 31 | 4 | 100 | 3 |

| England: 2nd innings | | | R | M | B | 4 | 6 |
|---|---|---|---|---|---|---|---|
| M. Trescothick | | b McGrath | 41 | 71 | 56 | 6 | 0 |
| A. Strauss | c Martyn | b McGrath | 106 | 246 | 158 | 9 | 2 |
| *M. Vaughan | c sub (Hodge) | b Lee | 14 | 45 | 37 | 2 | 0 |
| I. Bell | c Katich | b McGrath | 65 | 165 | 103 | 4 | 1 |
| K. Pietersen | lbw | b McGrath | 0 | 3 | 1 | 0 | 0 |
| A. Flintoff | | b McGrath | 4 | 20 | 18 | 0 | 0 |
| +G. Jones | not out | | 27 | 15 | 12 | 2 | 2 |
| A. Giles | not out | | 0 | 4 | 0 | 0 | 0 |
| Extras | (b 5, lb 3, w 1, nb 14) | | 23 | | | | |
| Total | (6 wickets dec, 61.5 overs, 288 mins) | | 280 | | | | |

DNB: M. Hoggard, S. Harmison, S. Jones.

FoW: 1–64 (Trescothick, 15.3 ov), 2–97 (Vaughan, 25.4 ov), 3–224 (Strauss, 53.3 ov), 4–225 (Pietersen, 53.5 ov), 5–248 (Flintoff, 59.1 ov), 6–264 (Bell, 61.1 ov).

| Bowling | O | M | R | W |
|---|---|---|---|---|
| McGrath | 20.5 | 1 | 115 | 5 |
| Lee | 12 | 0 | 60 | 1 |
| Warne | 25 | 3 | 74 | 0 |
| Gillespie | 4 | 0 | 23 | 0 |

| Australia: 2nd innings (Target: 423 runs) | | | R | M | B | 4 | 6 |
|---|---|---|---|---|---|---|---|
| J. Langer | c G. Jones | b Hoggard | 14 | 42 | 41 | 3 | 0 |
| M. Hayden | | b Flintoff | 36 | 123 | 91 | 5 | 1 |
| *R. Ponting | c G. Jones | b Harmison | 156 | 411 | 275 | 16 | 1 |
| D. Martyn | lbw | b Harmison | 19 | 53 | 36 | 3 | 0 |
| S. Katich | c Giles | b Flintoff | 12 | 30 | 23 | 2 | 0 |
| +A. Gilchrist | c Bell | b Flintoff | 4 | 36 | 30 | 0 | 0 |
| M. Clarke | | b S. Jones | 39 | 73 | 63 | 7 | 0 |
| J. Gillespie | lbw | b Hoggard | 0 | 8 | 5 | 0 | 0 |
| S. Warne | c G. Jones | b Flintoff | 34 | 99 | 69 | 5 | 0 |
| B. Lee | not out | | 18 | 44 | 25 | 4 | 0 |
| G. McGrath | not out | | 5 | 17 | 9 | 1 | 0 |
| Extras | (b 5, lb 8, w 1, nb 20) | | 34 | | | | |
| Total | (9 wickets, 108 overs, 474 mins) | | 371 | | | | |

FoW: 1–25 (Langer, 11.1 ov), 2–96 (Hayden, 29.4 ov), 3–129 (Martyn, 42.5 ov), 4–165 (Katich, 49.3 ov), 5–182 (Gilchrist, 57.4 ov), 6–263 (Clarke, 75.2 ov), 7–264 (Gillespie, 76.5 ov), 8–340 (Warne, 98.2 ov), 9–354 (Ponting, 103.6 ov).

| Bowling | O | M | R | W |
|---|---|---|---|---|
| Harmison | 22 | 4 | 67 | 2 |
| Hoggard | 13 | 0 | 49 | 2 |
| Giles | 26 | 4 | 93 | 0 |
| Vaughan | 5 | 0 | 21 | 0 |
| Flintoff | 25 | 6 | 71 | 4 |
| S. Jones | 17 | 3 | 57 | 1 |

**Result:** Match drawn
**Man of the Match:** R. Ponting
**Series:** Level at 1–1

# 6

———

I smiled at Trent Bridge. Yes, those of you who consider me the grumpiest man on the planet might require me to repeat that. I smiled. And what a brouhaha it caused.

It concerned, of course, the now infamous substitute story. Or non-story, as it should have been. But before I talk you through that, I just want to say that I am not grumpy. I might be considered a serious person, but the reason for my often stern gaze is hereditary. All my family have low jowls; just a slight lifting of them creates a smile. Happiness is in the heart – that might sound a horrible cliché – but it is true. And I could not be happier. And I do smile sometimes, as I proved here.

I smiled at Ricky Ponting. He didn't smile back. He was in a terrible temper for some reason. Quite why he was blaming me when his partner, Damien Martyn, had called him for a suicidal single to cover, I don't know.

You know what's more? All the palaver caused me to burn my

toast. Yes, that's right, it was the Saturday afternoon of the Test and I was making some toast in the main changing room. I heard the roar and looked up at the television. They showed the replay. Ponting had been run out by a long way. Fantastic. What a brilliant piece of fielding. 'What's wrong with Ponting? Why doesn't he want to leave the field?' I could hear people saying. I forgot about my toast and went out on to the balcony. There was an incident brewing. Ponting was nearing the boundary's edge, very obviously swearing and cursing. He looked up and began to direct his aggression towards me. I do not honestly know what he was saying, but it did not appear very friendly. I think that we can safely assume that he was abusing me. I altered my gaze towards the England players out in the middle to see what their reaction was. Then I glanced back down at Ponting. He was still ranting and raving. I did not want to be drawn into any sort of conflict, so I smiled. It only incensed him more. He could not take that. He completely blew his top. I did not actually think it at the time, but, looking back now, that might have been the moment when it became clear that England were going to reclaim the Ashes. This was an Australian side under enormous pressure. The mental strain was becoming so much that they were grasping any opportunity – however ludicrous – to hit back at us.

I might have smiled, too, because I found the whole scenario funny. There was no plan. I will state categorically here, in total honesty, that we did not have any preconceived or underhand plan to use substitutes so that we could rest our bowlers. We never have done. Never will. Ponting was clutching at straws. If he thought that he had a gripe, he chose the wrong moment to do it anyway. Durham's Gary Pratt, who effected the superb throw from cover, was on the field for Simon Jones. Jones was resting all right. He was in hospital, having an X-ray on an injured ankle for which he left the field after bowling just four overs in Australia's second-innings follow-on.

Let me tell you first how we select our substitute fielders. Phil Neale comes to me in April with a list showing which counties do not have any cricket during the Test matches. He asks me whether there are any players whom I would particularly like to have a look at. That is because sometimes we can use it as a facility to bring a Test hopeful into the dressing-room environment; to gauge his personality, his attitude, even his work ethic in and around the nets. I have done that on numerous occasions. The one I remember best was when I summoned Simon Jones up to Old Trafford for the Sri Lanka Test in 2002. That was interesting because there was a definite benefit to it. Not long before that I had happened to be down at Sophia Gardens watching Glamorgan play; in fact it was against the Sri Lankans in a tour match after the First Test, which had been drawn at Lord's. I was keen to see Jones bowl, because there had been some good talk about how he had performed at the National Academy that winter, and there was even a thought that we might consider him for the Second Test at Edgbaston. So I was somewhat taken aback to see how short his run-up was. I agreed that when I had been in my second season at Glamorgan in 1999 it had been far too long, but this was ridiculous. I reckoned that it needed to be about another five metres longer, and as chance had it, there was a pile of sawdust positioned right on the spot where I thought he should begin his run-up. I wish that I could have shouted out, 'Go back to the sawdust' but, of course, I couldn't. As I was thinking this, though, I was joined by Steve Watkin, Glamorgan's academy director and a bowling coach whom I rate highly. I asked him what he thought. He agreed entirely.

So it was not long afterwards that Jones came up to Old Trafford. I spoke to him about his bowling, and he admitted that he was lacking rhythm. 'I think you need to lengthen your run-up,' I told him.

'Are you sure?' he questioned. I could sense that he agreed with me but I said he should go back to Cardiff and speak with Watkin. 'If there are any questions, get Watty to phone me,' I told him, knowing full well that Watkin was on the same wave-length.

Again, by chance, I was down at Cardiff after that match and I saw Jones, who was talking with Lynn 'The Leap' Davies, the former Olympic long jump gold medallist, whom Jones had used a lot earlier in his career, especially to cure his no-ball problems. Davies also agreed that the run-up needed to be lengthened, and he should know – it is the same principle after all, of achieving sufficient momentum and rhythm before taking off behind a given line. So that is what Jones did. He made his Test debut against India at Lord's later that summer.

Anyway we have looked at many other players in the same manner. Paul Collingwood and Chris Tremlett for instance. Somerset's James Hildreth, who caught Ponting at Lord's in the First Test at backward point, was another. We also wanted to see

Middlesex's recently qualified Irishman, Ed Joyce, but he was unavailable. If there are no such players then Neale just asks the county uninvolved at that time to provide their two best fieldsmen. We do not take players out of county games to field for us. That would be nonsensical. If we are struggling sometimes, we then ask the MCC groundstaff if they can provide players.

When Worcestershire's Stephen Peters narrowly missed that run-out of Brett Lee on the last day at Old Trafford, some said that Collingwood should have been there. He was playing for Durham against Leicestershire, and rightly so. These players have to play too. They have their own professional careers to consider.

We were actually struggling to find suitable players for Trent Bridge, when Steve Harmison said, 'Pratty's not playing for Durham, give him a call.' He is a player we have used many times before and he is an excellent fielder, so we had no hesitation in doing so. When he turned up here he would have had no idea what was going to occur. Little could he have known that he would finish the summer riding on an open-top bus through London as we celebrated winning the Ashes.

We also called in Trevor Penney, Warwickshire's 37-year-old Zimbabwean. He is generally regarded as one of the best fielders to have graced the county game. I have heard the word 'genius' used in respect of his fielding. Now, tell me; if we had had a plan to put some brilliant fielders out there instead of our bowlers, would we not have put Penney out there first before Pratt? Of course we would.

I was told later that, soon after the Ponting incident, Penney too went out on to the field as a second substitute. I did not even realise that. It was certainly not my way of further winding up the Australians.

There were a couple of reasons why players were coming off the field during this series. The first was that some needed to relieve themselves. As simple as that. That would have represented 95 per cent of the occasions when a substitute was used, for no more than one over at a time. These days there is considerable emphasis placed by the physiologists on the correct levels of hydration. Everyone is encouraged to drink a lot, and obviously some have stronger bladders than others. It is not only the bowlers who come off. Marcus Trescothick and Michael Vaughan come off on the odd occasion, and we do not want such a good captain as Vaughan off for too long – not even for an over if we can help it. Amid all this fuss did anyone actually make a note of who was coming off each time and what for? Of course they didn't, except for two people – the umpires, who have to make a note of every coming and going in the course of their duties. Not once did they raise the issue with me or Vaughan. Therefore how have we been transgressing? A lot of people seemed to jump on the substitute bandwagon without having any knowledge of the full facts. But that is nothing new. There was some ridiculous statistic that England substitutes have taken more catches than those for any other country in the last four years, but what does that prove? Nothing.

Secondly there were some players who were coming off to see the physio. Some like Vaughan (knee) and Andrew Flintoff (ankle) have had surgery, and when a niggle develops in that same area it can cause concern. Most of the time they just want reassurance that it is not the same problem as that which necessitated an operation. In any case we would not want Flintoff off for very long – he is a brilliant slip fielder and you never see these substitutes fielding there, do you?

I would actually prefer it if the bowlers did not come off so often. They expend more energy running off the field, up the stairs, into the toilet and then back down the stairs than they would grazing at fine leg or third man. Anyway, in the 90 overs played in a day, what if players are off for a total of six or eight overs? It is nothing. It is no big deal.

This was not the first time that the Australians had raised this issue of substitutes. If you recall, John Buchanan had alluded to it during his rant back at me after the NatWest Series. They were not happy about the time spent on the field by Vikram Solanki as a substitute. To be honest, it was good to hear such comments. We could repel them with a clear conscience. We knew that we were doing nothing wrong.

Ponting was fined 75 per cent of his match fee for his outburst. But still he had not had enough. Speaking on a Melbourne radio station, this is what he said: 'I think it is an absolute disgrace [that] the spirit of the game is being treated like that. Fletcher has known right the way through the summer this is something we haven't been happy with, but it's continued. He knows it's something that has got under our skins and I've had enough of it, and I let him know that, and most of his players too. Being here in England they've obviously got the resources to just draft in the best fieldsmen that they possibly can at the time. The way they've been doing it is just before their bowlers are about to bowl; they'll send them off for a short amount of time to have a bit of a loosen-up and a massage and that sort of stuff, and come back on and bowl. As soon as they've finished their spell they'll do exactly the same thing. It's within the rules of the game but it's just not within the spirit of the game, which is what we're all trying to uphold.'

As I have explained, all of this is poppycock. At no stage of the series did any of our bowlers come off for a rub-down as Ponting suggested. But I thought it best that I did not react in any way to his comments. In fact I was pleased when David Morgan, the ECB chairman, later praised me for the manner in which I dealt with this situation. I could easily have blown this incident up, but to some degree I appreciated the stress and pressure Ponting was under. Indeed, before Ponting made those public comments I thought that the matter had been closed. The day after the incident I was walking down the stairs from the dining room at Trent Bridge when Ponting appeared coming the other way. As he came close I stopped and extended my hand, which he shook. I didn't say anything, but just nodded my head. My message was 'Let's shake hands on this and forget about it.' We went in our opposite directions and I thought that would be the end of it. Ian Bell happened to be walking behind me and he commented, 'That was a bit of a surprise.'

So too then were Ponting's later comments. Word also came back to me that there were some vitriolic comments being directed at me back in Australia. In fact so insulting were some of the remarks by one pair of radio presenters that I received a letter from an Australian lawyer offering to act against the defamation of my character. I seemed to have become the villain who had so wronged their captain. That could not be further from the truth.

What riled me most about Ponting's comments was his reference to the spirit of the game. Let us look at a number of incidents which had already occurred in the series and see whether the Australians were being so meticulous in their upholding of the spirit of the game.

First, amid all this talk of substitutes, what about the Old Trafford Test when Michael Clarke had his back problems? When he appeared to bat in the second innings, did he have a runner? No. Did he suddenly recover that morning then? Where was he when we were smashing it around the park the day before? I also noticed that Brad Hodge was on as a substitute fielder for him; that was strange when the Australians were also talking about it being traditional to use a bowler for twelfth man duties. Why was Mike Kasprowicz or Shaun Tait not on the field? It should be remembered that Hodge took two excellent catches, one at deep square leg in the first innings to dismiss Pietersen and the other at fine leg to end Vaughan's second innings.

Second – and this is the most serious example – whenever a decision went against Australia during the series, did you notice how Ponting would invariably walk straight up to the umpire and challenge his decision using overbearing body-language? On occasions, just like in football, he was supported by Adam Gilchrist. Sometimes there was even a third person involved. Is that really what we want kids to see when they watch cricket? Is that in the spirit of the game? Did you ever see Vaughan or any of the England players challenge the umpire in that manner during the series?

Third, what about Gilchrist saying loudly so that the umpire could hear: 'We're owed one dodgy decision here, boys,' in the second innings at Trent Bridge? That was reported by Simon Hughes in his column in the *Daily Telegraph*, and was no doubt unearthed during his work as the analyst in the Channel 4 van. Is it in the spirit of the game to be saying things like that?

Fourth, what about one of the Australians deliberately bowling on a pre-cut strip before the start of play on one of the match days of the Trent Bridge Test? It was clearly a strip being readied for a Nottinghamshire match, while another one had been clearly designated on the edge of the square for the bowlers to practise on: that is the norm at all Test grounds. This petulant behaviour was no doubt the upshot of some comments made by the groundsman to the press before the Test, to which some of the Australians had taken exception. We also had it on good authority that the groundsman was verbally abused by some of those same Australian players.

Fifth – and this is nearly as important as the second instance – going back to the Second Test at Edgbaston, was it in the spirit of the game to try to ensure that an opposition player was fined? Simon Jones was fined 20 per cent of his match fee after pointing Matthew Hayden to the pavilion after he had him caught at slip by Trescothick for 31. But soon after that incident had occurred, when the fourth umpire came through the dressing rooms from the field after a drinks break, there were Australian players bringing it to his attention. 'Make sure that you report it to the match referee,' was what they were suggesting.

Finally, was it not the Australians who were warned twice for slowing the game up on the fourth day at Old Trafford as we chased runs for a declaration and they were hoping to bowl as few overs as possible? Is that in the spirit of the game?

The shame was that all this fuss at Trent Bridge might have detracted from a magnificent game of cricket. When I went to the press conference after that third day all the questions concerned substitutes. Never mind that Australia had followed on for the first time in seventeen years and were 222–4 in their second innings. Maybe the Australians wanted something to deflect from that unwanted bit of history that they were creating.

It had been another good toss for Vaughan to win and yet again Andrew Strauss and Trescothick got us off to a rollicking start. Glenn McGrath was missing with an elbow problem, but, as I mentioned before, I did not consider that a significant factor. The openers put on 105 before Strauss was most unfortunate to be dismissed. I thought that Shane Warne had had some luck at Old Trafford with the manner in which he had snared Trescothick for that 600th Test wicket, but this was just as fluky. As Strauss swept Warne, he got a bottom edge which hit his boot and then bounced up high to Hayden at slip. That is pure misfortune. I heard afterwards that some commentators were berating Strauss for playing the sweep shot; no surprise there, given my previous mentions of their myopia on that subject. It was, in fact, good cricket because Warne had moved his field so that there was no one fielding at 45 degrees. Strauss was trying to manoeuvre the field around. As I mentioned earlier, we talk about this a lot because if you can force the opposition to place a man there then it takes him out of the game, opening up vast areas in front of the bat.

I have also heard that the Australians have said that they had no luck in this series. Well, there already you have two instances of where they had a large dollop of fortune. Had they also forgotten the rain that saved them at Old Trafford? The rain also helped them here. It definitely disrupted our momentum and rhythm on a first day which was reduced to 60 overs. Indeed Trescothick was out for a good 65 to the first ball after one rain break, bowled by a decent in-swinger from the debutant Tait. Interestingly I had gone to him and Vaughan just before they went back on to the field and warned them that there was a possibility that the ball might start swinging around. It is OK my saying that, though; what do you do first ball? Play for swing or not? Credit must go to the bowler for a good delivery.

We ended the first day on 229–4, which was a rather delicate position in my view. Vaughan had also batted well for his 58, but he edged one off Ponting. Now that was a surprise to see Ponting bowling his medium pace. We never thought that we would see that in the series: I might even have to admit that I did not have any plans in place to combat him. Despite Vaughan's demise, we could only see it as a positive, though. For the skipper to have to resort to bringing himself on showed that our batsmen had some measure of the Australian bowlers. They bowled a lot of no-balls (22 on that first day) and with one of them Trescothick – on 55 – was bowled by Brett Lee. There were also two dropped catches on that first day, hinting at a lack of precision from the Australians, which could only please us.

We had an important team chat before the start of play on the second day. We reminded them that 400 would be a good score. That was what we were aiming for; in order to do that, I thought that we needed two good partnerships, one of 70 and one of 50. The other four wickets would be able to muster the 60 or so required for our target.

Kevin Pietersen fell early, but that brought Geraint Jones to the wicket to join Flintoff. In such an enthralling series, with so many twists and turns, it is not easy to look back and pinpoint the most crucial moments. But if somebody said to me that this was the most crucial partnership of the series then I could not disagree. It certainly was up until that point. They put on 177. Only Hayden and Justin Langer put on more in the series – 185 in the first innings at The Oval – but that did not preface victory, so it gives you some idea what this partnership meant. It also meant that we scored 477 – 77 sweet runs more than we had planned for.

Flintoff scored 102 off 132 balls. I have little hesitation in stating that it was his finest innings for England. It oozed quality and class, and, coincidentally, announced him as a truly world-class all-rounder, by dint of his batting average now rising above his bowling. Anyone still labouring under that silly misconception that Flintoff was nothing more than a random big-hitter – a rough-hewn bully – were quickly disabused of that notion. He can now read match situations very cleverly, managing his risk assessment so that he can eventually hurt sides, regardless of the state of the game when he first comes to the crease. To score a Test hundred against Australia is special enough, but to do so in these circumstances, under this pressure, showed sheer class and nerve.

Let's not forget Jones either. I thought that he had kept excellently on the last day at Old Trafford – his reflex catch to dismiss Warne after a rebound off Strauss at second slip was brilliant – but still there was enormous pressure on him. His response was just as we would expect from him: full of character and resolve. That's why we pick him. He was playing on Chris Read's home ground too, the man many seem to think should be playing instead of him.

There was also pressure on Matthew Hoggard. As you may have noticed that I quite like to say, he had not 'come to the party' hitherto in this series. Trent Bridge, since the building of the new stand there, has a reputation for swing. So everyone was saying 'Hoggard will have his chance now'. In some eyes it was even considered his last chance; a tad harsh when one considers that it was only seven months previously that he was taking 12–205 in a man-of-the-match performance against South Africa at the Wanderers. He had also been man-of-the-match for his 8–97 against Bangladesh at Durham. He might have bowled, by his own admission, like a 'trollop' against outclassed opposition, but it was still Test cricket and not very long ago. Some people have very short memories.

We like to say that we 'cover all bases' with our bowling attack. This was a classic example of what we mean by that. There was no internal pressure on Hoggard. He knows his role within the bowling attack. There are always going to be certain conditions in which some struggle, others when some will excel. That is cricket. And so he responded superbly by taking three early wickets to help reduce Australia to 99–5 by the close of day two.

A word about Vaughan's captaincy here, too. When he took Harmison off after his opening spell, it would have been easy to have just turned to Flintoff, our most attacking and aggressive bowler. Instead he called upon Simon Jones, whom he thought might be more dangerous in the swinging conditions. That was quality decision-making. But even then he always needs the bowler to back up his judgement. And Hoggard and Jones did that, using those conditions to their considerable advantage.

It had been an incredible day's play; we were heavily in the ascendancy. But I went to bed that night knowing that a crucial decision might have to be made the next day. To make Australia follow-on or not?

There was a lot of talk about it. At Old Trafford we had decided not to enforce it because the bowlers had spent a long time in the field. Here we had only bowled 30.3 overs overnight. If we bowled them out for 150 we would definitely make them follow-on. If it was for 200, then the situation became a little less clear.

But first we had to bowl Australia out. Cue some swinging magic from Simon Jones. He took three wickets in fifteen balls, bowling a spell of 5.1–1–22–4 that morning, to end up with 5–44 and confirm, if there was any doubt, that he is now a bowler transformed; a bowler at home in the highest company. The ball with which he bowled Mike Kasprowicz was a pearler, starting as if it was going to duck into the batsman and then curving sharply away to bowl him neck and crop.

As for that catch of Strauss's at slip to remove Gilchrist – it was absolutely stunning. His left hand became a telescope. The catch of the series, no doubt. He was, though, brought crashing back to earth later in the day when he grassed Langer on 37. So often cricket does that to you.

Australia 218 all out then, and 259 behind. Vaughan had come off the field not long before (to relieve himself, in case you are wondering), and asked me in passing about the follow-on: 'What do you think I should do?'

'What do you want to do?' I replied.

'I want to make them follow-on,' he said without hesitation.

'Do it then,' I said, 'but just ask the bowlers first. Make sure that they want to do it.' They did.

We obviously would not have done so if we had known that Jones was going to pull up lame with his ankle injury. He bowled just those four overs in the second innings before limping off. I think that we would have bowled Australia out for less than 300 in that second innings if he had been fit, even though it was a very flat pitch.

As it was, I was worried that anything over 100 would be difficult to chase. And that is not an assessment made with the benefit of hindsight. I told the rest of the back-up team so on that Saturday. For rather obvious reasons I did not tell the team.

For the record, Ponting had scored 48 when he was run out by Pratt. He had looked good, too. But he was betrayed by an awful call from Martyn. There was never a single there – the television replays showed me that as I was making my toast. I do not miss many balls live though; that was a rarity. I'm pictured enough times, impassive and inscrutable on the balcony, to verify that.

All credit to the rest of the bowling attack, who so manfully stuck to their task without Jones, eventually dismissing the Australians for 387, leaving us 129 to win. Ashley Giles, especially, came back well after not bowling as he might have liked on the last day at Old Trafford.

There were more missed chances – there were a lot on both sides in this series, for some reason. One of the reasons I would give for that is the sheer volume of cricket played at present. Such is the intensity that it is difficult for the players to maintain their concentration for such long periods of time. There will inevitably be mistakes. On the Saturday evening Geraint Jones missed a stumping, but this was much harder than the one which had reprieved Shane Warne in Manchester. He was blinded, as Alec Stewart was quick to point out to me after play that day: 'I can see how he missed it,' he told me.

And on the fourth afternoon Pietersen dropped another catch, his sixth of the series. By now I had picked up on a technical flaw, but I wanted it confirmed. Trevor Penney was sitting with me. I said to him, 'Right, I will watch the batsman and call when he hits the ball. You tell me what sort of position KP is in as the ball is hit.' We did that, and my hunch was right. It is all to do with Pietersen's excitability, as I said earlier. Basically he is rushing in as the bowler runs in, but is not then setting up a base for himself when the ball is hit. His head is not still, with eyes level, at the critical moment. That is a must, whether batting or fielding. Your head has to be still.

Cricketing traditions are now being challenged on this issue. As a youngster you are always told to walk in with the bowler. That is fair enough, but what you must do is then adopt a position similar to that of a football goalkeeper when a penalty is about to be taken. You must be on your toes with a solid base so that you can spring off in either direction or even upwards if required. You probably only need to take a couple of steps before you do that. What Pietersen was doing was finding himself on one leg as the ball was hit. There was no base from which to pounce. That is why he dropped Kasprowicz here. The ball was hit above his head at mid-wicket but he was not able to get that far off the ground because of his unbalanced starting position.

It is a problem that Pietersen will correct, though. He is a wonderfully natural athlete, but it will require some practice. I once read somewhere that, for every day that you execute a skill wrongly, it takes nigh on ten days to put it right. So it will not be as simple as you might think. But he will sort it.

Could we sort it to chase 129 to win, though? I always thought so. As I said, I knew it was going to be difficult but I never thought we would lose; my only real jitter came when Flintoff was out at 103–5. I was so confident that I was thinking, 'If we played out this chase five times, we should win three of them by five wickets, and the other two by seven or eight wickets.' It clearly got a bit tighter than that, but I probably should have factored in the drama which this series had already brought. Nothing was going to come easily.

The start was the key; Trescothick and Strauss were marvellously positive and we had 32 on the board before we lost a wicket. In my book Trescothick was the unsung hero of this series. He came into it with the Australians thinking that they had worked him out, but he coped with that pressure, and ended up with 431 runs at 43.10. His intent was clear throughout the series and he set down a marker for the rest of the batting order to follow.

Here his upbeat tempo sent out an even more powerful message to the Australians. The quick start meant that Warne could not attack as much as he would have liked from the beginning of his spell. Warne was obviously the danger man. It might have been an option to open the bowling with him, but I suppose that the seamers had to be given an opportunity first. I'm actually glad that they were.

Warne really is a champion. The characteristic which distinguishes him from all other bowlers down the ages is his ability to change so smoothly and quickly from attacker to defender. From over the wicket to round the wicket. No other bowler has been able to do that. Not even Muttiah Muralitharan. He just wears you down.

The pitch was still flat, with only Flintoff receiving a ball which deviated significantly from the main part of the strip, the nip-backer from Lee being an absolute beauty. But the problem lay with Warne pitching in the foot-holes outside the right-handers' leg stump. The ball which accounted for Vaughan turned sharply from that area.

Matters were becoming very tense in the dressing room. As a

little partnership was being built, you could sense the players becoming boisterous. Then a wicket would fall and silence would descend. As the next partnership was gradually being built, the noise levels would begin to creep up again. The players think that they have got it bad in terms of pressure, but what about me? I cannot even do anything about the situation. That is the gist of what I said to Ashley Giles when he came into the coach's room, which is alongside the main dressing room on the top floor of the Trent Bridge pavilion. We were four wickets down and he already had his pads on. Normally he would be the most relaxed of characters, but he was very nervous here. 'I'm not sure how I am going to cope,' he said to me.

'At least you are one of the players who can do something about this. Once you cross that line, you will be fine,' I told him. 'It is programmed into you. This is why you practise so hard – for situations like this.'

I also had to speak to Hoggard. With any batsman you do not want to complicate his mind by cramming it full of too many instructions. So I said, 'Just look to score off the seamers. Don't even try to score off Warne.' That is what he did, hitting a full toss from Lee through extra cover for four on his way to the most important 8 not out of his life. He has worked so hard at his batting with Phil Neale over the years – exactly what we have always wanted from our lower order – that it was almost fitting that he was there at the end. It used to be that Hoggard was number eleven and that the groundsman used to start up his roller when he went out to bat. Not any more.

Moments later Giles, another who has justified our insistence on the lower order being capable of contributing with the bat, clipped Warne through mid-wicket for the winning runs. We had won by three wickets. Another cliff-hanger, but we were 2–1 up, with one to play. I think I smiled again, but nobody seemed to notice this time.

## Fourth Test

*England v. Australia*
*Trent Bridge, Nottingham*
*25–28 August 2005*

**Umpires:** Aleem Dar (Pak) and S. Bucknor (WI)
**Toss:** England

| England: 1st innings | | | R | M | B | 4 | 6 |
|---|---|---|---|---|---|---|---|
| M. Trescothick | | b Tait | 65 | 138 | 111 | 8 | 1 |
| A. Strauss | c Hayden | b Warne | 35 | 99 | 64 | 4 | 0 |
| *M. Vaughan | c Gilchrist | b Ponting | 58 | 138 | 99 | 9 | 0 |
| I. Bell | c Gilchrist | b Tait | 3 | 12 | 5 | 0 | 0 |
| K. Pietersen | c Gilchrist | b Lee | 45 | 131 | 108 | 6 | 0 |
| A. Flintoff | lbw | b Tait | 102 | 201 | 132 | 14 | 1 |
| +G. Jones | | c & b Kasprowicz | 85 | 205 | 149 | 8 | 0 |
| A. Giles | lbw | b Warne | 15 | 45 | 35 | 3 | 0 |
| M. Hoggard | c Gilchrist | b Warne | 10 | 46 | 28 | 1 | 0 |
| S. Harmison | st Gilchrist | b Warne | 2 | 9 | 6 | 0 | 0 |
| S. Jones | not out | | 15 | 32 | 27 | 3 | 0 |
| Extras | (b 1, lb 15, w 1, nb 25) | | 42 | | | | |
| Total | (all out, 123.1 overs, 537 mins) | | 477 | | | | |

FoW: 1–105 (Strauss, 21.4 ov), 2–137 (Trescothick, 30.5 ov), 3–146 (Bell, 34.1 ov), 4–213 (Vaughan, 55.2 ov), 5–241 (Pietersen, 64.1 ov), 6–418 (Flintoff, 103.2 ov), 7–450 (G. Jones, 112.5 ov), 8–450 (Giles, 113.1 ov), 9–454 (Harmison, 115.1 ov), 10–477 (Hoggard, 123.1 ov).

| Bowling | O | M | R | W |
|---|---|---|---|---|
| Lee | 32 | 2 | 131 | 1 |
| Kasprowicz | 32 | 3 | 122 | 1 |
| Tait | 24 | 4 | 97 | 3 |
| Warne | 29.1 | 4 | 102 | 4 |
| Ponting | 6 | 2 | 9 | 1 |

| Australia: 1st innings | | | R | M | B | 4 | 6 |
|---|---|---|---|---|---|---|---|
| J. Langer | c Bell | b Hoggard | 27 | 95 | 59 | 5 | 0 |
| M. Hayden | lbw | b Hoggard | 7 | 41 | 27 | 1 | 0 |
| *R. Ponting | lbw | b S. Jones | 1 | 6 | 6 | 0 | 0 |
| D. Martyn | lbw | b Hoggard | 1 | 4 | 3 | 0 | 0 |
| M. Clarke | lbw | b Harmison | 36 | 93 | 53 | 5 | 0 |
| S. Katich | c Strauss | b S. Jones | 45 | 91 | 66 | 7 | 0 |
| +A. Gilchrist | c Strauss | b Flintoff | 27 | 58 | 36 | 3 | 1 |
| S. Warne | c Bell | b S. Jones | 0 | 2 | 1 | 0 | 0 |
| B. Lee | c Bell | b S. Jones | 47 | 51 | 44 | 5 | 3 |
| M. Kasprowicz | | b S. Jones | 5 | 8 | 7 | 1 | 0 |
| S. Tait | not out | | 3 | 27 | 9 | 0 | 0 |
| Extras | (lb 2, w 1, nb 16) | | 19 | | | | |
| Total | (all out, 49.1 overs, 247 mins) | | 218 | | | | |

FoW: 1–20 (Hayden, 9.3 ov), 2–21 (Ponting, 10.3 ov), 3–22 (Martyn, 11.1 ov), 4–58 (Langer, 19.3 ov), 5–99 (Clarke, 30.3 ov), 6–157 (Katich, 39.2 ov), 7–157 (Warne, 39.3 ov), 8–163 (Gilchrist, 42.2 ov), 9–175 (Kasprowicz, 43.2 ov), 10–218 (Lee, 49.1 ov).

| Bowling | O | M | R | W |
|---|---|---|---|---|
| Harmison | 9 | 1 | 48 | 1 |
| Hoggard | 15 | 3 | 70 | 3 |
| S. Jones | 14.1 | 4 | 44 | 5 |
| Flintoff | 11 | 1 | 54 | 1 |

| Australia: 2nd innings (Following on) | | | R | M | B | 4 | 6 |
|---|---|---|---|---|---|---|---|
| J. Langer | c Bell | b Giles | 61 | 149 | 112 | 8 | 0 |
| M. Hayden | c Giles | b Flintoff | 26 | 57 | 41 | 4 | 0 |
| *R. Ponting | run out (sub [Pratt]) | | 48 | 137 | 89 | 3 | 1 |
| D. Martyn | c G. Jones | b Flintoff | 13 | 56 | 30 | 1 | 0 |
| M. Clarke | c G. Jones | b Hoggard | 56 | 209 | 170 | 6 | 0 |
| S. Katich | lbw | b Harmison | 59 | 262 | 183 | 4 | 0 |
| +A. Gilchrist | lbw | b Hoggard | 11 | 20 | 11 | 2 | 0 |
| S. Warne | st G. Jones | b Giles | 45 | 68 | 42 | 5 | 2 |
| B. Lee | not out | | 26 | 77 | 39 | 3 | 0 |
| M. Kasprowicz | c G. Jones | b Harmison | 19 | 30 | 26 | 1 | 0 |
| S. Tait | | b Harmison | 4 | 20 | 16 | 1 | 0 |
| Extras | (b 1, lb 4, nb 14) | | 19 | | | | |
| Total | (all out, 124 overs, 548 mins) | | 387 | | | | |

FoW: 1–50 (Hayden, 13.4 ov), 2–129 (Langer, 33.6 ov), 3–155 (Ponting, 44.1 ov), 4–161 (Martyn, 46.1 ov), 5–261 (Clarke, 94.2 ov), 6–277 (Gilchrist, 98.5 ov), 7–314 (Katich, 107.3 ov), 8–342 (Warne, 112.3 ov), 9–373 (Kasprowicz, 119.2 ov), 10–387 (Tait, 123.6 ov).

| Bowling | O | M | R | W |
|---|---|---|---|---|
| Hoggard | 27 | 7 | 72 | 2 |
| S. Jones | 4 | 0 | 15 | 0 |
| Harmison | 30 | 5 | 93 | 3 |
| Flintoff | 29 | 4 | 83 | 2 |
| Giles | 28 | 3 | 107 | 2 |
| Bell | 6 | 2 | 12 | 0 |

31. Matthew Hayden claims a bizarre catch off the bowling of Warne, second right, as the ball ricochets off Andrew Strauss's right boot. We batted first again and made 477, our highest total of the series.

. Marcus Trescothick ushes a delivery from ee away to leg during his first-innings 65.

33. Freddie on his way to a superb 102. This Ashes series established him as the best all-rounder in the world.

34. The catch of the series: Strauss somehow extends his body to seemingly twice its nor
length to pouch an edge from Gilchrist. Flintoff, the bowler, looks suitably amazed.

35. In Australia's first-innings
reply, Brett Lee top-scored with
47 off 44 balls. Their total of
218 all out was not enough to
avoid the follow-on, the first
time they had been asked to do
so since 1988.

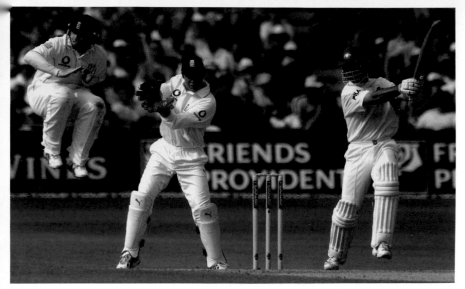

36. Ian Bell takes evasive action as Ponting cuts during Australia's second innings.

37. But soon afterwards England were celebrating Ponting's dismissal, run out the substitute fielder Gary Pratt, here congratulated by Geraint Jones.

38. Australia's captain had chuntered about our use of substitutes throughout the series and here has words with Matthew Hoggard before trudging off – and then making his feelings known to me on the balcony.

39. Jaffa. With Australia all out for 387, our target was just 129 to win – but we had to work for every run, as Warne caused problems and Lee bowled quickly and aggressively. Here he bowls Flintoff for 26 with a beauty, leaving us 111 for 6.

40. But Giles and Hoggard see us home, with Ashley hitting the winning runs to put us 2–1 up in the series and needing only a draw at The Oval to reclaim the Ashes.

Discussing tactics with Andrew Flintoff before the crucial Fifth and final Test.

With rain forecast, the weather would also be a factor. Here Michael and I assess the ditions.

43. Andrew Strauss on his way to 129 during the first day of the Fifth Test.

44. The Oval crow salutes Ashley Gil fine catch to see o Brett Lee and brir Australia's innings an end, just six ru short of England's total.

45. Matthew Hoggard (4 for 97) and Andrew Flintoff (5 for 78) leave the field on the fourth day after Australia had slumped from 323–3 to 367 all out.

46. Cometh the hour, cometh the man. What a time to make a maiden Test hundred. Kevin Pietersen's crucial 158 in our second innings saw us through to safety and series victory, scoring priceless runs and taking up valuable time.

The champagne moment – Michael Vaughan and the team celebrate the series victory regained the Ashes for England.

48. Ashley Giles kisse[s] the urn in the dressin[g] room after the final [day] at The Oval.

49. Harmison and Flintoff enjoy a cold beer and a well-earned rest at the end of a long and exhausting summer. Between them they'd taken 41 Australian wickets.

50. Coach and captai[n]. Managing director an[d] consultant. Moments don't come much swe[et] than this. We've done [it].

| England: 2nd innings (Target: 129 runs) | | | R | M | B | 4 | 6 |
|---|---|---|---|---|---|---|---|
| M. Trescothick | c Ponting | b Warne | 27 | 24 | 22 | 4 | 0 |
| A. Strauss | c Clarke | b Warne | 23 | 68 | 37 | 3 | 0 |
| *M. Vaughan | c Hayden | b Warne | 0 | 8 | 6 | 0 | 0 |
| I. Bell | c Kasprowicz | b Lee | 3 | 38 | 20 | 0 | 0 |
| K. Pietersen | c Gilchrist | b Lee | 23 | 51 | 34 | 3 | 0 |
| A. Flintoff | | b Lee | 26 | 63 | 34 | 3 | 0 |
| +G. Jones | c Kasprowicz | b Warne | 3 | 25 | 13 | 0 | 0 |
| A. Giles | not out | | 7 | 30 | 17 | 0 | 0 |
| M. Hoggard | not out | | 8 | 20 | 13 | 1 | 0 |
| Extras | (lb 4, nb 5) | | 9 | | | | |
| Total | (7 wickets, 31.5 overs, 168 mins) | | 129 | | | | |

DNB: S. Harmison, S. Jones.

FoW: 1–32 (Trescothick, 5.1 ov), 2–36 (Vaughan, 7.1 ov), 3–57 (Strauss, 13.5 ov), 4–57 (Bell, 14.1 ov), 5–103 (Pietersen, 24.1 ov), 6–111 (Flintoff, 26.4 ov), 7–116 (G. Jones, 27.6 ov).

| Bowling | O | M | R | W |
|---|---|---|---|---|
| Lee | 12 | 0 | 51 | 3 |
| Kasprowicz | 2 | 0 | 19 | 0 |
| Warne | 13.5 | 2 | 31 | 4 |
| Tait | 4 | 0 | 24 | 0 |

**Result:** England won by 3 wickets
**Man of the Match:** A. Flintoff
**Series:** England leads 2–1

# 7

I had never felt like this before. It was the morning of Monday, 12 September; the final day of the Fifth Test. The day on which the Ashes were to be decided.

A good night's sleep had not been a problem in our splendid Grange City Hotel near Tower Bridge. And having breakfasted alone – as usual at about 7 a.m., earlier than most of the squad or management team – I was feeling comfortable considering what lay ahead that day.

I walked to the lift, waited and then got in, pressing the button for the top floor. As the lift went up, my mind began skirting to the day ahead. It was a big day, certainly – the biggest in my time as England coach – but we would be OK. The lift opened and it was a short walk back to my room. But it was then that something happened. Something strange. It hit me. Suddenly at that moment the magnitude of this day must have come crashing into my body. I began retching. 'Crikey, what's going on here?' I

155

thought. This was one of the few occasions in my life where my nerves were getting the better of me. My pace quickened down the passageway. I eventually got into the room. My wife, Marina, knew there was something wrong. 'What on earth is the matter? Are you OK?' she asked concernedly.

'I need something to chew on,' I said. 'I don't know how I'm going to be able to clean my teeth.' That was a funny thing to be considering at that moment but it was indicative of the way I was feeling. It was a bizarre experience. Thankfully it passed quickly. As soon as I left the room to go to the ground, it had gone. I felt fine. I had to. I had to be in control by the time that I saw the players. They would be nervous enough as it was. I have always prided myself on being able to maintain an even keel as a coach, irrespective of the set of circumstances that might be unfolding before me and the team. This was no time to be changing that. And to think that at that stage I had not even realised how much winning the Ashes might mean to the whole nation. I knew how much it meant to the team and the English cricketing fraternity – I outlined that at the start of the book – but as for the wider conscience of the whole nation; not really. I had some inkling but no real comprehension. That would come later.

That Monday was no normal day, but then again, this had been no normal Test match and no normal build-up. It is not every day that you are mistaken for Richie Benaud. That happened to me on the Tuesday before the Test, at a dinner organised for Mark Butcher's benefit year. As I was sitting at my table next to Matthew Maynard, a lady collecting autographs approached. 'Mr Benaud?' she said. As I turned towards her, it suddenly dawned on her that I was not Richie Benaud. 'Oh, you're not Mr Benaud,' she said, rather embarrassed.

'He's over there,' I said, pointing to his table. She certainly did not want my autograph. I hope that she was not intimating that I should be retiring like the great man did at the end of this game – from British television anyway. At least he will continue to commentate in Australia.

But, of course, Maynard thought this was hilarious. He just could not stop laughing. Nor blabbing either. For within minutes the whole room seemed to know about this *faux pas*. It was no surprise when it appeared in the *Daily Telegraph* a couple of days later.

In its own small way that dinner did reveal a snippet of how much this Oval Test match meant. I say small, but there were probably over 500 guests there. And when the auction bid for an individual to have his photograph taken with the England squad (who were all there) rose to many thousands of pounds, then it started to come home to me that this was a Test match which might be a little different from the others in which I had ever been involved.

Even though I tried to immune myself from all this hype, I had other worries. I had done since the end of the Trent Bridge Test, in fact. About selection, that is. It had not been an issue since the First Test; the selectors had picked the same eleven for four Tests. But now with Simon Jones nursing an ankle injury, that seemed about to change. That was a shame because I was told that the last time England had gone through an entire series with the same eleven had been way back in 1884/85, when

Arthur Shrewsbury's team won 3–2 in Australia. I suppose that I should have known that such good fortune was never going to last. But at least it was a far cry from my previous Ashes experiences. All those injuries I mentioned earlier meant that in 2002/03 we used seventeen players for the Tests. In 2001 we had had to call on nineteen, all because of injuries again. Mind you, look back to 1989 and 1993, when they selected twenty-nine and twenty-four players respectively, and you can see that these are much more stable days. If the players are picked correctly in the first place, then I think that we have shown that consistency of selection bears fruit.

Of course, when we met to select the squad for The Oval, we did not know for definite that Jones wasn't going to make it. But we had a fair idea. And, in any case, I always think that it is best to prepare yourself for the worst case. That way there is no panic if that scenario reveals itself.

So who to include should Jones not pass muster? There was no obvious candidate; no stand-out fast bowler in county cricket shouting out his claims to be picked. That was disappointing in a way. We had held high hopes for Chris Tremlett but there were just too many question marks hanging over him. He was not bowling well, which was probably a result of not having bowled enough. And there were concerns over a knee niggle which he had been carrying for a while. Regardless of any of this, was it just too important a match to be bringing in a debutant? It probably was.

There were a couple of older bowlers whom we might have looked at, but both Darren Gough and Andrew Caddick were injured. Caddick, especially, would have been a front-runner. He might have lost some pace since his best days but he can still swing the ball and make it bounce. Imagine how he might have been as a second change bowler in this Test. He would have been ideal. As for Gough, you can say that he had officially retired from Test cricket. But I know him; he would have been at The Oval like a flash if we had told him that he was required.

I phoned all those usual points of contact when I am struggling with a selection decision – Nasser Hussain, Mike Atherton and Alec Stewart, to name three – but there was no clear favourite emerging to replace Jones. I decided to phone Butcher, not necessarily for his advice on whom to select, or to say that I was able to make it to his dinner, but rather to pick his brains on how the Oval pitch had been playing during the season. He is Surrey captain after all, even if that wrist injury had kept him out for most of the season. He told me that every type of bowler had struggled there during the 2005 season; it had been a very good pitch on which to bat, apparently. But there was one thing he mentioned which set me thinking; which suddenly gave me a handle with which to work. 'Azhar Mahmood has been able to reverse-swing it,' he said, 'sometimes as early as the fifteenth over.' In one way it only made me yearn more for Jones to recover his fitness, but in another it told me that if we were going to play an out-and-out fast bowler instead of Jones, then it had to be someone who could use reverse swing effectively. My mind immediately turned to James Anderson; he had performed such a role for us before. There was still, of course, the option of playing Paul Collingwood, but we will come to that.

Lancashire's Anderson had been a bowler we had been discussing anyway. I decided to phone his county coach, Mike
Watkinson. I had heard that Anderson, like all the Lancashire
bowlers, had been struggling to find his conventional swing, but
what about the reverse?

'Has he been reverse-swinging it?' I asked Watkinson. Yes,
came the reply. It is my view that in order for reverse swing to be
effective, the ball needs to be propelled at 85mph, at the very
least. Anderson can do that. That was it in my mind, then.
Anderson had to be in the squad. And I was convinced more
than ever that, when in a quandary, if you ask enough knowl-
edgeable cricket people, something will come out of the
woodwork. Butcher had proved that. Until I had spoken to him,
I had been floundering.

There was a persuasive argument in favour of Collingwood,
though. He had done well in the one-day matches against the
Australians and I had long suspected that they do not like his
attitude. He is very good at 'getting in their space' – that phrase
again. He also has an unremitting desire to play regular Test
cricket for England, which manifests itself in his boundless
energy whenever he appears in the Test squad.

But he was not the only one in that sort of mood when we
arrived at The Oval for practice on the Tuesday. So was everyone
else. They were all well rested, even those whom I had permitted
to play in the C&G Trophy final, namely Kevin Pietersen, Ian
Bell and Ashley Giles. I had no problem with that. The Trent
Bridge Test had finished on the Sunday and there had not been
back-to-back games, as there had been when I made the decision

about the C&G Trophy semi-finals. And for those who might have been worried, Michael Vaughan's benefit match at Headingley was rained off.

The practice went really well. At the back-end of a series you are always worried about how much benefit players are gleaning from a particular practice, concerned that a 'Groundhog Day' mentality could easily creep in. You try and vary things as much as you can; different warm-ups, different fielding routines and so on. But here we decided that we should stick to our normal routines. It was a big enough game without the players being alerted even more to that fact by unnecessary changes to their routine. Just like the players, I look in the mirror too and will walk away from a practice, asking myself: 'Did I do a good enough job there? Did they really benefit from that?'

I think that they did here. In fact Troy Cooley and Maynard both mentioned independently that they thought it had gone really well. There was a lot of laughter and I could sense a real eagerness to get on with the game. There was no fear of this huge challenge. With their attitude and demeanour the players were saying to me: 'Bring it on.' I had spoken to them before practice about their mental attitude. It was a similar chat to the one I had used at Trent Bridge. There, I told them that I had never doubted their technical abilities; that I knew that they could match the Australians in that respect, but the biggest test of the summer had been whether they could match them mentally. They had proved beyond doubt that they could do that already, but it was not an area where they could now slacken off. That mental attitude had to be spot-on. We talked again of making history, as we had done many times before. But this was this team's opportunity to make their biggest piece of history yet.

Now we had to decide upon the final eleven. There were various permutations. For it was not just a straight choice between Collingwood and Anderson, as everyone assumed. We did, in fact, briefly discuss omitting Ian Bell and playing the pair of them. That would have meant promoting Kevin Pietersen to four, having Collingwood at five and Andrew Flintoff at six. But that was soon shelved. For the reasons, see above; that consistency of selection again.

As regards Anderson, there was still a nagging concern at the back of my mind about how he had done in his last Test – against South Africa at the Wanderers. There we had brought him in to replace Simon Jones because we felt that his conventional swing would be more use. Of course, Jones's conventional away swing has since improved markedly, but Anderson struggled a little there. It is always a big ask for a young bowler to perform in a one-off situation like that. And it might be the same here at The Oval.

We still have a high regard for Anderson, and he has a big international future, but I was veering towards Collingwood. So it seemed was Vaughan, as we talked at practice on the Wednesday. Then suddenly Collingwood was hit while batting in the nets. Quite a nasty blow, too. We had seconded a couple of West Indian quickies to bowl at practice and one of them had bounced Collingwood, who was a little late on his hook shot. It went through the grille and hit him smack on the nose. For a moment it looked serious. 'Bang go all our selection thoughts,' I said to myself. But he was OK. I should have known that really. As I said, he is not the sort of character who is going to let something like that force him out of a Test match. After all, he had only played two Test matches before this (both on the tour to Sri Lanka in 2003) and had long wanted to buck that reputation of just being a one-day specialist. This was an opportunity he was not going to spurn. And I thought it right that he should play. The all-round package which he offers to the team is so impressive, and Vaughan concurred too.

If there had been some initial indecision about that, there was certainly none about what to do if we won the toss. Bat first, no doubt about that. That would mean that we would have batted first in four out of five Tests, even if one of those (Edgbaston) had been at Ricky Ponting's bidding. And thankfully that is what happened.

It is OK winning the toss, but then you still have to ensure that you make the most of doing so. At 319–7 at the end of the first day's play I felt that we probably had not done ourselves justice. Looking back, the players themselves would probably admit that there had been too many soft dismissals. Although they did say that the pitch was not as flat as might have been expected; more like a pitch of day two than day one, and exceptionally dry. But, credit where credit is due, there had also been some excellent batting. Andrew Strauss made a composed century, his second of the series and the seventh in his young Test career; I wonder if Shane Warne regrets calling him 'the new Daryll' after his archbunny, South African Daryll Cullinan, earlier in the series. Strauss and Marcus Trescothick again gave us a romping start, putting on 82 in little more than seventeen overs at just under five runs an over. Throughout the series we scored at 3.87 runs per over; that's pretty impressive stuff.

In the field placings for Trescothick there was further confirmation of how the mental balance of superiority had shifted. This was the batsman whom the Australians previously thought was an expert at giving slip-catching practice, yet here he was very early in his innings facing Brett Lee with just two slips in position. And this on a bouncy pitch and with the ball swinging too. Australia had obviously come over with plans to implement for each batsman, but as the series had unfolded, they found themselves increasingly unable to stick to these. Vaughan had been able to do that. It was a crucial element to the series.

Another element which was becoming more and more obvious was that any England innings in this series was being played in two parts. The first was against the quicker bowlers and involved mostly quick scoring. The second began as soon as Warne was introduced to the attack. That was when batting became much more arduous. But this was a process to which we were accustomed. It is even more pronounced whenever you play against Sri Lanka; batsmen must cherish that period before the unique talents of Muttiah Muralitharan enter the fray. And when Warne and Muralitharan do enter the attack, the other bowlers can feed off them, utilising the pressure which those two can create. The mental psyche of the batsman is altered considerably and he understandably becomes more cautious against the other bowlers, even if he had been comfortable against them before the introduction of Warne or Muralitharan.

Warne was on by the fourteenth over here. He bowled 34 overs on the first day, finishing with 5–118. We hoped that we had tired him out so much that he might not be as effective later in the match. No chance of that, though, with this tireless maestro.

Our chat at the start of day two naturally revolved round our ambition to reach 400. Remember those goals we set at the start of the summer? Four hundred in the first innings of the Test was the crux of the batting goal. And nothing had changed here. That was what I emphasised to the players. It is now traditional that I speak to them on days one and two of a Test, Maynard on day three and Cooley on day four. Before Maynard joined the management team, it was me on days one, two and three, and then Cooley on the fourth. If the match goes to five days, then it is up to me to finalise who speaks on that last day. Those chats always take place before practice begins; assuming a 10.30 a.m. start, that is at 9 on the first day and at 9.15 on the others. Vaughan will have had his big chat with the team on the night before the Test, and he will also speak to them in a huddle after they have gone on to the field of play. Sometimes he will ask other players to speak in that huddle – in fact I do not know one player who has not done it at some stage. This is all part of the greater plan to charge everyone – both the players and the coaches – with responsibility at some stage. As I have already touched upon, there are not too many people in life who throw away responsibility; those who do are rarely possessed of sufficient character to succeed. Now it was my job to try to cajole the remaining batsmen sufficiently (Geraint Jones and Giles were not out overnight) so that they took responsibility to ensure that we had a total which might put the Australians under pressure.

We did not reach that figure of 400, but, still, 373 was a competitive total. And we competed on that second morning. Jones was bowled by a good ball from Brett Lee which held up on him, but Giles (32) and Matthew Hoggard (only 2, but he lasted 36 balls) battled hard and Steve Harmison added some vital late blows in a breezy 20 not out.

Before this Test Australia's best opening stand of the series had been 58 in the first innings at Old Trafford, but Justin Langer and Matthew Hayden surpassed that comfortably here by reaching 112–0 at tea on that second day. That stand probably said more about the flatness of the pitch than our bowling. It was looking a much better pitch than we had envisaged. But then the openers accepted the offer of the light from the umpires. That surprised me, as it did everyone else. I thought that they might have carried on a bit longer, and that meter reading then set a precedent for the rest of the match, with rain eventually ending the proceedings for the day. It was gloomy but this was a side which needed to win to keep the Ashes. They did not portray themselves as such with this decision.

What really interested me about their innings was the manner in which they set about Giles. As soon as he was introduced to the attack Langer went for him. Giles conceded fourteen in that over but there were a couple of risky shots, one of which only just cleared long-on. To me it was a demonstration of how effective Giles has become; that they looked to attack him so eagerly and quickly. This was a side who knew that he played a vital role.

Coach John Buchanan had drawn attention to it at the start of the series, saying that he thought we used Giles just to tie up an end while resting the quicker bowlers, and that they had to get at him so that Vaughan would be forced into bringing back the fast men sooner. There is an element of that in Giles's role, but he is a better bowler than he is often given credit for. Australia know that, deep down.

Cleverly, Vaughan changed his end immediately, so that Giles could bowl to a longer boundary. There he could come into his own as usual, bowling tightly, but not as negatively as many suppose. Sure, he did not take any wickets but he was assuming a role which the Australians did not like. Here they wanted to hit him out of the attack even more keenly than usual because we were without Simon Jones. They wanted to get at Collingwood. Then they would try to hit him just as hard so that the quicker bowlers would have to be reinstated before they had rested sufficiently.

Collingwood did bowl, and took a few people by surprise, probably including Trescothick who missed a chance off Langer at slip. It seemed to beat him for pace. We had been telling Collingwood for a long time that he needs to bowl at a speed of at least 80mph, so it was pleasing to see that the speedometer was regularly reading over that in this game. One ball touched 83mph which shows good improvement for a man who used to bowl at little more than 78mph.

If the tensions of the match were not enough, we were all then incensed by some external comments, of which we became aware on the Friday. They were made by Malcolm Speed, the chief executive of the ICC. Speaking in reply to a question on Radio Five Live about our use of substitutes during the summer, he said, 'I think Ricky Ponting has a point there. We need to be careful that we keep it under control, define what's acceptable and that the captains buy into that.'

Basically we thought that he was taking sides in this issue, which I found very disconcerting in the middle of such an important Test match.

This was not the first time I had been perturbed by remarks made by an ICC official. In 2003 former Indian batsman Sunil Gavaskar made some particularly derogatory comments about the England team's performances in the recently finished series in India. He had described our approach as only being 'good for people suffering from insomnia', also saying: 'Thank God it was a three-Test series and not a five-Test one, for Indian cricket would have lost a great number of spectators seeing the fare dished out. Why our cricket board are keen on having a five-Test series when England visit India next is beyond comprehension for, without the slightest doubt, they are the most unattractive and boring side to have played cricket in India.'

This was strong stuff from Gavaskar. Completely unjust and out of order, though. I thought that we had done well in that three-Test series in India, which we had lost 1–0 with an under-strength side. So when I was asked for a comment about these remarks in Hamilton, New Zealand, where we travelled for the second half of that winter, I said just two things: 'First, it's very important to realise that he's on the ICC panel and should have an unbiased opinion; and second, it's very sad when a good wine goes sour.' I was very disappointed with Gavaskar. He was a cricketer for whom I had always had the utmost respect when I was playing. Often I would be asked who was the greatest player I had played against, and while I never thought I could answer that, I always said that Gavaskar was the one for whom I had the greatest amount of respect. As well as in India, he had scored hundreds away from home, and especially in the West Indies, where a lot of players who have been termed 'great' have struggled. He also scored all his runs without a seam attack to back him up, and that is important in my view, because it's all very well doing it when you have some quick men to bully the opposition. But after these comments, which I think might have been made because he had a problem with the English press rather than the cricket team, I lost respect. He had not recognised how well we had played in India, especially as we were missing so many key players.

Back at The Oval by the end of another rain-affected third day Australia were 277–2; a slightly worrying state of affairs in some ways but, knowing the way this series had gone and the character of the individuals involved, not one which was irretrievable. It was not an easy day coming on and off regularly, with play divided up into five sessions rather than three. But sometimes that can actually help the bowlers in that they are always fresh. If I was being really mischievous I might suggest that it would not have been a surprise if the Australians had claimed some double-dealing with the weather gods to ensure that our bowlers could be well rested every time they began a spell. But I won't.

What I will say is that Flintoff bowled quite superbly. I was going to say that he bowled with the heart of a lion. That would be wrong. Three lions more like. On that Saturday he had figures of 12.4–5–28–1. He just kept pounding in. The ball was mostly damp so there was little swing, either conventionally or in the reverse manner. So he relied on seam movement and bounce. And, of course, raw pace. It is at this juncture that I would like to proffer a small question. Do you think Flintoff would have been able to run in with such venom and hostility in the Fifth Test of such an exhausting series, if he had not been rested earlier in the season? I don't think he would. You make your own judgement. Whatever you decide, though, remember that you are acting with the benefit of hindsight. I have to make those sorts of decisions in the middle of the summer. I have to look ahead to the end of the series and attempt to gauge how tired players might be then. Contrary to some opinions, I do not enjoy pulling players out of county cricket. But I do have to plan ahead.

I know that I keep harking back to the issue of mental tiredness – and apologies for the repetition – but I have to say that I have never seen a side so mentally focused as the England eleven in this final Test. That chat on the Tuesday before the game had not fallen on deaf ears. Yes, it was probably the biggest game of their lives, but there were signs aplenty to me that the pressure of that was being channelled in the right directions. Normally in the last Test of the summer there is much talk of the winter ahead; there was none here. I can scarcely remember Pakistan or India being mentioned.

That mental fortitude came to the fore on the fourth day. To bowl Australia out for 367 – a lead of six runs – really was a remarkable achievement. Even I did not think that we would do that. To think that Australia lost their last 7 wickets for 44 runs in 90 balls – that gave us a huge psychological lift. Flintoff was again supreme, on this day bowling unchanged to record figures of 14.2–3–30–4. He ended with his second five-wicket haul in Test cricket; the hugely impressive statistics reading 34–10–78–5. In conditions which were now suiting swing as well as seam, Hoggard was no less penetrative, ending with 4–97. So his series yielded sixteen wickets at an average of 29.56. His strike rate of 45.8 was actually better than that of Flintoff (48.5) and Harmison (56.8). For those wondering, a bowler's strike rate is the average number of deliveries before he takes a wicket. Simon Jones was England's best in this series with 34.0.

The weather was closing in again, though, and it was fairly obvious that bad light was going to play its part when we batted for a second time. Lee bowled just one over before being taken off, which allowed Warne to snare Strauss to leave us 2–1. But the skipper came in and showed positive intent with Trescothick, as we reached 34–1 by the early close. One day to go and we were 40 ahead with one wicket down. The match could hardly have been more delicately balanced. It was understandable that it was going to be a nervous night for everyone. I just never expected myself to be quite so affected by events.

A couple of peripheral matters were already worrying me, though. First, it had become public knowledge that there was going to be an open-top bus parade in London should we regain the Ashes. Trafalgar Square had been booked, apparently. I was not particularly enamoured of this. I do not like tempting fate and I always feel that such announcements can only add further motivation to the opposition, however small. I know that if I had been the opposing coach in this instance I would have mentioned this at some stage.

Second, it had been decided that we should travel to The Oval on the last day by bus. 'Why the big deal?' you might well ask. Well, usually during home Tests we all travel in our own cars to the grounds. Everyone seems to like that tiny bit of independence which you simply cannot have when you are abroad on tour. But it was a departure from the norm which troubled me a little. I could see the reasoning – whatever the result it was likely (and only right and proper) that the players would want to have a drink afterwards – but still it made me a touch anxious.

But by bus it was, and this was it. The final day of the Fifth Test. The destination of the Ashes boiled down to this one day. I sensed something slightly different about the atmosphere in the dressing room before we went out to warm up. Normally there is a lot of noise with players congregated in groups. Here, everyone seemed to be on their own; alone with their thoughts. But we had to alter that. We had to try to treat it like any other day of Test cricket. That is not easy under such pressure, but it is the only way to deal with big days like this. Build up the importance of the day and it can only spell trouble. Even from the practice on the Tuesday before the match we had been trying to avoid that. That is why I had been worried about the bus journey to the ground that morning. It had signalled that this was no ordinary day.

The team talk was simple. Vaughan had shown the way on Sunday evening; we had to be positive. That had been our successful method throughout the summer, and this was no time to be changing that. Forget about those stone-walling glories of days gone by. We had seen at Lord's in the First Test what could happen if we became too defensive in our batting mindset. I told the team that I thought that we needed two partnerships, one of 75 and one of 50. It was a deliberately low, but eminently realistic target, so that the players did not feel under that much pressure.

I talked the talk, but it was Vaughan who walked the walk immediately; our symbiosis revealed. He had admitted himself that his dismissal in the first innings – chipping a Warne short delivery to mid-wicket – had been a little soft, but his 45 here was worth many, many more. It set the tone, as did Trescothick's 33, before Vaughan was out to a good delivery from Glenn McGrath.

That brought in Ian Bell, who fell first ball to the same bowler; a pair for the unfortunate young man. I felt for him – that is not a nice experience at any level, let alone in such an important match. But I would have liked to have seen any other right-hander play that ball first up. It was a very good delivery. I looked at it again later on the Feedback Analysis video screen and it confirmed what I thought I had seen at real-time pace: it stopped and held off the pitch from a very awkward length. It is exactly the sort of delivery a right-hander does not want first ball. Much was made of the fact that Bell managed to reach double figures on only three of his ten visits to the crease during the series, but if I am honest, I would be more concerned if he was being dismissed frequently between 20 and 30. That is always of more concern as a coach, when a batsman is wasting a good start. Anybody can get out early between 0 and 10, especially in Test cricket where the bowling is naturally of the very highest standard. Somebody mentioned afterwards that another England player bagged a pair when England won a series 2–1 against South Africa in 1998 – Flintoff. That is not a bad omen. Bell will come good.

In came Pietersen, with McGrath on a hat-trick. There was a huge appeal first ball but the ball hit his shoulder rather than glove. He was also dropped on nought when an edge off Warne hit Adam Gilchrist's gloves and ricocheted on to Hayden's leg with him unable to react in time. And he was also dropped by Warne off Lee when he had only 15. So, yes, he had some luck, but so do a lot of batsmen when they score runs. That is part of cricket. I only mention them here because I think that too much was made of them at the time. I heard that some people were going around saying, 'Warney's dropped the Ashes.' There were a lot of other incidents during the series which might have contributed to the end result, you know.

But as Pietersen said afterwards, 'Shane Warne dropped me, but then I've dropped six catches this series. I'll take the hundred.' To be exact he scored 158 off 187 balls with seven sixes (a record in an Ashes Test, surpassing Ian Botham's six at Old Trafford in 1981) and fifteen fours. It was an incredible knock. He had been a little miffed before the game because of comments made by Geoff Boycott and Mike Gatting, saying that he was 'getting ahead of himself' and what-not. So this was the perfect response. In fact he ended up ahead of everyone else – in the series run-scoring stakes, that is. His 473 topped the charts, followed by Trescothick (431) and Flintoff (402). Langer (394) pipped Strauss (393) by one run, otherwise we would have had the top four.

If there was any doubt – and there was not in my mind – that Pietersen was a player born to excel under the most pressurised of environments, then this expelled it. You can tell that he is a special cricketer. Whenever he walks out to bat I do not think that there is anyone in the England dressing room who does not say, 'I'm going out on to the balcony to watch this.' There are not that many players in world cricket about whom you can say that. You can even see his effect when we are having net sessions. Players will stop what they are doing and watch him. He is a wonderful role model in that respect. The manner in which he works at his game in the nets is a lesson to any aspiring young cricketer. He does not just go in there and hit balls randomly like some players. He goes in with an express purpose and practises certain shots, hitting the ball into certain areas. People can say what they like about his off-field life but he is a top professional when it comes to the cricket side of things.

When Flintoff hit one back to Warne for eight, we were 126–5 just before lunch and I was fretting a little. Not that I could show it. I never can. I never will. That is my mantra as coach. I thought all along that if we could reach 250, then it would be an interesting game. We might even have been in a position to win it because Australia would have been duty-bound to chase any target which was presented to them. And they have never had a good record of chasing smallish totals. Nonetheless I was thinking, 'I would rather that they didn't have that opportunity right now.' I am all for positive, entertaining cricket but this was no time to be setting up a thrilling last afternoon run chase. The crowd would have their fill of excitement and enjoyment anyway.

Collingwood was the next man in. Having missed the four previous Tests it cannot have been easy for him in this Test. You miss all the build-up and then you are suddenly plunged into this inferno of pressure and expectation. Mentally it must have been so hard for him to adjust to the intensity of this match. He had played in the one-dayers but this was something very different.

He scored 10. Forget what I said earlier about ensuring that the batsmen were positive in their outlook. Collingwood assessed the situation and realised that it required some good old-fashioned crease occupation. His innings lasted 72 minutes and 51 balls and, in my opinion, he played Warne superbly. He cannot have ever scored a more valuable ten runs. While he was taking up precious time, Pietersen was launching a withering attack at the other end, especially upon Lee, whose plan to bowl short only resulted in thirty-seven runs being haemorrhaged in three overs.

Collingwood could, however, do little about the delivery with which Warne dismissed him, bouncing and finding his glove before ballooning to Ponting at silly point. Geraint Jones soon followed and we were 199–7. Jitters again. Inside, that is. Not for anyone to see.

Who should come to the rescue? Ashley Giles. There is a

South African red wine I quite like, named 'Faithful Hound'. It reminds me of Giles. He is a wonderful professional and the success which came his way here could not have happened to a nicer guy. He added 109 with Pietersen to kill off any hope Australia had of snatching victory in this match. That eighth-wicket alliance was the highest at The Oval against Australia; all that talk about creating history and this was an opportune occasion to be making a small note in history amid the greater achievement. Giles's 59 was his highest Test score. He had scored the winning runs at Trent Bridge; now he saw us to safety. He had had all those detractors early in the series. He had probably said some things that he wished he hadn't. But now some were saying that it was Ashley Giles who won the Ashes for us. That is some sweet turnaround.

Once we passed 280 I felt safe. It was time to relax a bit. Pietersen went when we had made 308. It fascinates me that he made the same score as Basil D'Oliveira did in that history-changing Test on the same ground in 1968. That is almost spooky.

We were eventually all out for 335, but right until the end we were winning mini-battles. Australia missed a trick. Lee had bowled with real hostility at Hoggard but when the light became too murky they decided to turn again to Warne. He finished with 6–124, giving him forty wickets for the series. But if Australia had continued with their barrage of bouncers we might have been forced to go off for bad light – there would have been no point risking injury at that stage – presenting them with a minor moral victory, in that we would have regained the Ashes by accepting the bad light. Instead, by acting as they did, they then had to go and bat. They needed 342 off 18 overs. And as soon as Harmison began bowling short in his first over, they accepted the offer of the light. It might seem a trivial matter, but for me it was our final act of one-upmanship in the series. We had won a series of minor skirmishes which all added to the winning of the major battle. Is that not what war is all about? The players must have felt like they had been in a war by the end.

At 6.15 p.m. (on Monday, 12 September 2005 – I wanted to mention it again because I shall never forget it) umpires Billy Bowden and Rudi Koertzen walked out to the middle and removed the bails. That was it. We had done it. All that work, all that planning, all that worry, all that heartache – even feeling a little sick that morning. It had all been worth it. After 16 years and 42 days of Australian occupation, England had at last regained the Ashes. It was time for some celebratory chaos.

## Fifth Test

*England v. Australia*
*The Brit Oval, London*
*8–12 September 2005*

**Umpires:** B. Bowden (NZ) and R. Koertzen (SA)
**Toss:** England

| *England: 1st innings* | | | R | M | B | 4 | 6 |
|---|---|---|---|---|---|---|---|
| M. Trescothick | c Hayden | b Warne | 43 | 77 | 65 | 8 | 0 |
| A. Strauss | c Katich | b Warne | 129 | 351 | 210 | 17 | 0 |
| *M. Vaughan | c Clarke | b Warne | 11 | 26 | 25 | 2 | 0 |
| I. Bell | lbw | b Warne | 0 | 9 | 7 | 0 | 0 |
| K. Pietersen | | b Warne | 14 | 30 | 25 | 2 | 0 |
| A. Flintoff | c Warne | b McGrath | 72 | 162 | 115 | 12 | 1 |
| P. Collingwood | lbw | b Tait | 7 | 26 | 26 | 1 | 0 |
| +G. Jones | | b Lee | 25 | 60 | 41 | 5 | 0 |
| A. Giles | lbw | b Warne | 32 | 120 | 70 | 1 | 0 |
| M. Hoggard | c Martyn | b McGrath | 2 | 47 | 36 | 0 | 0 |
| S. Harmison | not out | | 20 | 25 | 20 | 4 | 0 |
| Extras | (b 4, lb 6, w 1, nb 7) | | 18 | | | | |
| Total | (all out, 105.3 overs, 471 mins) | | 373 | | | | |

FoW: 1–82 (Trescothick, 17.3 ov), 2–102 (Vaughan, 23.5 ov), 3–104 (Bell, 25.6 ov), 4–131 (Pietersen, 33.3 ov), 5–274 (Flintoff, 70.1 ov), 6–289 (Collingwood, 76.3 ov), 7–297 (Strauss, 79.4 ov), 8–325 (Jones, 89.3 ov), 9–345 (Hoggard, 100.2 ov), 10–373 (Giles, 105.3 ov).

| *Bowling* | O | M | R | W |
|---|---|---|---|---|
| McGrath | 27 | 5 | 72 | 2 |
| Lee | 23 | 3 | 94 | 1 |
| Tait | 15 | 1 | 61 | 1 |
| Warne | 37.3 | 5 | 122 | 6 |
| Katich | 3 | 0 | 14 | 0 |

| *Australia: 1st innings* | | | R | M | B | 4 | 6 |
|---|---|---|---|---|---|---|---|
| J. Langer | | b Harmison | 105 | 233 | 146 | 11 | 2 |
| M. Hayden | lbw | b Flintoff | 138 | 416 | 303 | 18 | 0 |
| *R. Ponting | c Strauss | b Flintoff | 35 | 81 | 56 | 3 | 0 |
| D. Martyn | c Collingwood | b Flintoff | 10 | 36 | 29 | 1 | 0 |
| M. Clarke | lbw | b Hoggard | 25 | 119 | 59 | 2 | 0 |
| S. Katich | lbw | b Flintoff | 1 | 12 | 11 | 0 | 0 |
| +A. Gilchrist | lbw | b Hoggard | 23 | 32 | 20 | 4 | 0 |
| S. Warne | c Vaughan | b Flintoff | 0 | 18 | 10 | 0 | 0 |
| B. Lee | c Giles | b Hoggard | 6 | 22 | 10 | 0 | 0 |
| G. McGrath | c Strauss | b Hoggard | 0 | 6 | 6 | 0 | 0 |
| S. Tait | not out | | 1 | 7 | 2 | 0 | 0 |
| Extras | (b 4, lb 8, w 2, nb 9) | | 23 | | | | |
| Total | (all out, 107.1 overs, 494 mins) | | 367 | | | | |

FoW: 1–185 (Langer, 52.4 ov), 2–264 (Ponting, 72.2 ov), 3–281 (Martyn, 80.4 ov), 4–323 (Hayden, 92.3 ov), 5–329 (Katich, 94.6 ov), 6–356 (Gilchrist, 101.1 ov), 7–359 (Clarke, 103.3 ov), 8–363 (Warne, 104.5 ov), 9–363 (McGrath, 105.6 ov), 10–367 (Lee, 107.1 ov).

| *Bowling* | O | M | R | W |
|---|---|---|---|---|
| Harmison | 22 | 2 | 87 | 1 |
| Hoggard | 24.1 | 2 | 97 | 4 |
| Flintoff | 34 | 10 | 78 | 5 |
| Giles | 23 | 1 | 76 | 0 |
| Collingwood | 4 | 0 | 17 | 0 |

| England: 2nd innings | | | R | M | B | 4 | 6 |
|---|---|---|---|---|---|---|---|
| M. Trescothick | lbw | b Warne | 33 | 150 | 84 | 1 | 0 |
| A. Strauss | c Katich | b Warne | 1 | 16 | 7 | 0 | 0 |
| *M. Vaughan | c Gilchrist | b McGrath | 45 | 80 | 65 | 6 | 0 |
| I. Bell | c Warne | b McGrath | 0 | 2 | 1 | 0 | 0 |
| K. Pietersen | | b McGrath | 158 | 285 | 187 | 15 | 7 |
| A. Flintoff | | c & b Warne | 8 | 20 | 13 | 1 | 0 |
| P. Collingwood | c Ponting | b Warne | 10 | 72 | 51 | 1 | 0 |
| +G. Jones | | b Tait | 1 | 24 | 12 | 0 | 0 |
| A. Giles | | b Warne | 59 | 159 | 97 | 7 | 0 |
| M. Hoggard | not out | | 4 | 45 | 35 | 0 | 0 |
| S. Harmison | c Hayden | b Warne | 0 | 2 | 2 | 0 | 0 |
| Extras | (b 4, w 7, nb 5) | | 16 | | | | |
| Total | (all out, 91.3 overs, 432 mins) | | 335 | | | | |

FoW: 1–2 (Strauss, 3.4 ov), 2–67 (Vaughan, 22.4 ov), 3–67 (Bell, 22.5 ov), 4–109 (Trescothick, 33.1 ov), 5–126 (Flintoff, 37.5 ov), 6–186 (Collingwood, 51.5 ov), 7–199 (Jones, 56.5 ov), 8–308 (Pietersen, 82.5 ov), 9–335 (Giles, 91.1 ov), 10–335 (Harmison, 91.3 ov).

| Bowling | O | M | R | W |
|---|---|---|---|---|
| McGrath | 26 | 3 | 85 | 3 |
| Lee | 20 | 4 | 88 | 0 |
| Warne | 38.3 | 3 | 124 | 6 |
| Clarke | 2 | 0 | 6 | 0 |
| Tait | 5 | 0 | 28 | 1 |

| Australia: 2nd innings (Target: 342 runs) | | R | M | B | 4 | 6 |
|---|---|---|---|---|---|---|
| J. Langer | not out | 0 | 3 | 4 | 0 | 0 |
| M. Hayden | not out | 0 | 3 | 0 | 0 | 0 |
| Extras | (lb 4) | 4 | | | | |
| Total | (0 wickets, 0.4 overs, 3 mins) | 4 | | | | |

DNB: *R. Ponting, D. Martyn, M. Clarke, S. Katich, +A. Gilchrist, S. Warne, B. Lee, G. McGrath, S. Tait.

| Bowling | O | M | R | W |
|---|---|---|---|---|
| Harmison | 0.4 | 0 | 0 | 0 |

**Result:** Match drawn
**Man of the Match:** K. Pietersen
**Series:** England won 2–1
**Player of the Series:** A. Flintoff (Eng) and S. Warne (Aus)

# 8

The night on which we won the Ashes, I was in bed by 10.30 p.m. Even my wife, Marina, returned to the hotel later than me. She had been out with the wives and girlfriends of all the other players and management squad.

How sad and boring, I can hear some of you saying. How typical. I don't mind. I actually think it is funny. I have been ribbing Marina about her late return ever since.

But there is actually a more serious point to be made here: namely that the wives and girlfriends having such a good evening was an illustration of a crucial factor in the make-up of this successful England team. Their friendly togetherness helps create an environment that this is one big family. Because that is what it is. They are a welcome part of what I call the team 'bubble'. And the team performs all the better for it. I think the partners suffer more under the pressure than we do. They seem to play every ball with us and suffer every anxiety. No wonder that they were also ready to have a good night out on that Monday. They deserved it as much as we did.

Except, of course, that I did not actually have a night out. Not as such. I celebrated, though. In the dressing rooms at The Oval. We did not leave there until around 10 p.m.

But before we come to that, let's go back to the moment of glory and the rather odd events which preceded it. At 5.59 p.m. the Australian openers accepted that offer of the light. Everybody knew England had now won the Ashes. They had actually known that for probably an hour at least. It would be quite interesting to look back and try to pinpoint exactly when the moment came, but I suspect it would be far too subjective an exercise. As I said, I thought 280 was the cut-off score. Others might think differently.

No matter. But the frustrating thing was that the draw still could not be finally confirmed. Cricket's archaic and inflexible laws and regulations mean that the game could not be called off immediately. There was nothing to play for, nothing to be gained by any more cricket being played. There was a full house waiting to celebrate England's first Ashes triumph since 1986/87. And yet we were all left to wait around. I wouldn't say that it put a dampener on proceedings because it would have taken something seismic to mar such a momentous occasion, but it was an unnecessary irritation. Common sense should have prevailed and the game called off as a draw as soon as Hayden and Langer left the field. But no.

There is a solution to this. A simple one in my view, and it is a proposal I have previously outlined to the ICC. The match referee should be given more power, a wider brief. This goes back to my experiences in the business world. In my opinion, every international tour should be seen as the opening up of a business venture in that country. And the match referee should be the chief executive of the commercial enterprise. So before the tour starts, he should be sent ahead to check things out, just as you would in any business. Everyone should report to him – whether they are umpires, coaches, captains, groundsmen or local officials. He should be in charge of the net facilities and the match pitches that are prepared, including the warm-up matches.

During my time as England coach we have had countless rows on tours about the standard of practice facilities. People always think that we are being unnecessarily niggly whenever we complain about such things, but they should remember that international cricketers deserve a certain standard of practice facility; at least three decent nets with net bowlers provided, and a bowling machine too. But complaints of this nature should always be made to the match referee. As things stand, they are not. There are too many administrative meetings with local officials which can create bad feeling. The match referee should be able to take control of all such matters and in doing so would nullify much of this ill-will which is only natural when a touring side is critical of its host's facilities.

Here at The Oval the match referee (the Sri Lankan Ranjan Madugalle) should have possessed the power to call the game off. When the Australians accepted the umpires' offer, he could have spoken to the umpires by walkie-talkie and told them it was off. It would have been so much better if the players could have then walked off knowing it was all over. They even sat on the edge of the outfield for a moment before the umpires told them to move up to the dressing rooms. It was all a little strange.

Enough of my carping. The match was eventually declared a draw and the bails were lifted by the umpires. Mayhem ensued. The Oval went mad. And quite right, too. There was much shaking of hands, hugging and all those usual mannerisms of a side which has achieved something great. I don't think that is a gratuitous use of the word. What we had achieved was, indeed, something worthy of the adjective 'great'. We sang our team song as well. It was the loudest and most passionate rendition yet. Naturally so in the circumstances. Mind you, there was so much noise outside that it was doubtful whether we could be heard by anyone. Not that ease on the ear or even ensuring that the opposition hear it are the specified purposes of the song. It is our special celebration of a win; something to make the players feel proud of their team and what it has achieved.

Sorry to disappoint you, but I am going to struggle to describe the feeling in the dressing room immediately afterwards. How can you put something like that into words? It was emotional, for sure. You may at times have heard retiring professional sportsmen talk of how much they are going to miss the dressing room when they have finished. That might be a little difficult to comprehend for those who have never experienced the unique camaraderie engendered in the dressing room of a professional sports team. Sure, there is a special bond in any team sport, but professionals naturally spend more time together, and especially cricketers, for whom the length of actual playing time is obviously so much longer than other sports. That creates something a little different. Most of all, they miss moments like the one we were experiencing here at The Oval.

Having said that, though, this was something different again from any other celebration I had experienced in professional cricket. But even before we began celebrating in the dressing rooms this day had bucked a trend. Immediately after the draw had been confirmed, there were the presentations to be made on the outfield. I had a dilemma here. Never before had the off-field management team been involved in these. In general I do not believe that they should be. It is the players who should lap up the glory when they win. Remember that I only consider myself a consultant to the team. If a business has done well you would not see its consultant conspicuously basking in its success, would you? He would have done his job behind the scenes and that would be that.

But the problem was that I knew that quite a few of my management team wanted to go down on to the outfield and be a part of the celebrations. I could understand that. It was a day like no other, after all. I also knew that if I said that I was not going to go down and join in, then they would not want to go down without me. That is how loyal they are. So I decided to break the golden rule and go down. I immediately felt better about doing so when, as we were all descending the steps from the dressing room, Michael Vaughan shouted: 'I want all the management team on the stage with the team.' To me that demonstrated the close relationship which had been fostered between the players and the back-up staff. Despite my obvious unease it made me feel very good deep down.

I felt most uneasy when everyone was bouncing around on the stage. That just did not feel right at all for me. But I enjoyed the lap of honour around the ground. It was incredible to think that it must have been nearly an hour after the game had finished and yet not a soul seemed to have left the ground. Nobody wanted to leave.

After that, though, I decided that it was time for me to make my exit. I was the first one of the England entourage back up the steps into the dressing room. I sat there on my own for a few minutes. I really enjoyed that. It afforded me just those few precious moments to reflect and attempt to take in the magnitude of what had just happened. It wasn't easy to do that, but I tried. And then the rest returned: noisy, boisterous, happy, exultant, and desperate to get drunk. They were all of these and much more. And why not? I was soon hearing of plans for the night out, players challenging each other in drinking contests. Enjoy it, boys, enjoy it.

We all went into the Australian dressing room for a drink. I'm not sure why we did that, because it is normally the losing side which goes into the winners' dressing room. And before you say it, it was not because we were so used to losing to Australia at the end of a series that we did it out of habit. That was not the case. Most definitely not the case. We knew that we were deserved winners. And they did, too. As Simon Jones was to say quite memorably the next day: 'We done 'em.'

It was nice to sit and chat with the Australians. They were very hospitable and friendly, and it was obvious that both sides had got on well during the series. I did not stay for too long. I had a few glasses of wine, but not too many. There were a few matters to sort out, so I went back to our dressing room. There were players flitting back and forth between the two rooms all night. Well, we were not there all night, as I said, but it seemed like it. I just don't know where the time went. It flew. Suddenly the call went up that it was time to board the bus. I was glad that we had a bus now. No one would have been in any state to drive. Not for a couple of days at least.

When we went out to the bus, there were still a good number of fans waiting outside for us. That really was magnificent. I would like to thank them. Not just them, of course, but all the fans who supported us during the summer. We are the best supported team in the world; I have no doubt about that. There a lot of people in England who are all too eager to knock the England cricket team, but in general the fans that turn up to the matches are fantastic. That is why we like the Barmy Army so much. They are so loyal to us. You will never hear them criticising us. That is why the team always goes to thank them.

The bus journey back to the hotel was brilliant, with lots of singing and happiness. Yes, pure and unadulterated happiness. That is what there was on that bus. It was magical. Maybe it was the alcohol, but I can recall and describe the feelings a lot more readily from that stage of the evening. Maybe earlier there had still been a bit of shock about what had happened, with people coming to terms with the win after a long and exhausting summer. Now there was not.

But when we got back to the hotel I just slipped quietly up to my room. Lots of players were trying to persuade me to join them, but I was just too tired. I knew that I would not last too long if I went out. I felt good enough inside. There was a warm glow of satisfaction. I thought I would leave it at that.

By all accounts most of the players extended their celebrations a little further than I did. Some were said not to have made it to bed at all. It did not bother me in the slightest. They had every right to drink as much as they wanted. Anyone criticising them for doing so was just being prudish.

The only problem was that we had the open-top bus parade the next morning. I thought that was a little unfair on the players after their heavy night. A day off then the parade on the Wednesday would have been ideal. I bet that when the England rugby team won the World Cup in 2003, they celebrated just as long and hard as this group of cricketers. It was just that their parade was not the next day. Mind you, they were a few thousand miles from London at the time.

I felt sorry for Phil Neale. He had so much organising to do. And before the Test had finished, all he got from me was comments like: 'It's not over until the fat lady sings.' As I said earlier, I was distinctly uneasy over all these premature arrangements. But it was a decision which had long been taken out of our hands.

But it was on now. There was another minor debate: should Gary Pratt go on the bus? He had been a substitute at The Oval too and had celebrated hard with the team, but should he now join the team, even though he had never actually played for England? All the players were adamant that he should. They all emphasised the importance of the run-out of Ricky Ponting at

Trent Bridge. Pratt was coming then. 'Somebody find him some kit,' went the cry. Neale provided a shirt and Paul Collingwood a pair of trousers so that Pratt looked something like the rest of us, albeit without tie and blazer, which he obviously could not wear.

I was worried that the parade might be a flop. In my naïvety I was concerned that there would only be a few people lining the route as we went through London. As I said earlier I had no per-ception of what this victory meant to the wider public. I knew what it meant to beat Australia. Even growing up in Rhodesia (now Zimbabwe) it had been inculcated upon us that they were the team to beat, even more so than England. That might actu-ally sound strange, because it seems that everyone in the world always wants to beat England, but that is the way it was. That is why it was all the sweeter when my most memorable moment as a player came against them in the World Cup of 1983 as we defeated them at Trent Bridge by 13 runs. If you will permit, I'll brag for a short moment and tell you that I scored 69 not out and took 4–42 that day. It just took me a while – twenty-two years – to feel so good about beating them again.

But I had no idea that when we left the Mansion House in London that day that there would be people nine or ten deep waiting to applaud us – cheer, scream, wave and sing too. I kept looking into their eyes: in some of them there were tears of joy, in all of them was an enormous amount of pride. If I had known that there would be this sort of reaction if we won, then I might have been even more nervous before that last Test. Imagine what I might have been like on that last morning then?

On the route there were people from all walks of life, all age groups and from all over the world. At one stage I spotted a group of people, who looked like they were of Chinese origin, clapping and waving. That really surprised me. Now, I am not being prejudiced here, but that part of the world is not exactly renowned for its cricketing prowess or interest – were they just caught up in the emotion of the parade, or were they genuine supporters of cricket? It intrigued me. I think that I discovered the answer later. I told my son Michael about this. He worked for Surrey CCC last summer in their finance department and was at the final Test with his wife Cindy. He told me that lots of tickets had been sold to Chinese and Japanese fans, and he himself had seen a number there at the game, speaking in their native tongue. That is marvellous. It truly emphasised to me the effect that this series had had; how far it had reached.

Being in Trafalgar Square was almost an unreal experience. How did it happen that a boy from a modest farm just outside Harare could be here now? I had to pinch myself at times. And I was touched again by the loyalty shown by the skipper. It had been arranged that the team would sit at the front and the management team behind, but Vaughan said: 'No, I want Fletch sitting next to me.' That meant a lot. I think that the television people might have had to change their schedules, too, because of Vaughan's insistence that I be by his side. I don't think that I was supposed to be interviewed. Who said that I wasn't media-friendly?

The hymn 'Jerusalem' was sung. With much gusto, too. That made me smile. When it had first been introduced at cricket grounds in England it had produced a lukewarm response. People said that it would not catch on. Now, after this success it was different. For that is what it takes. If the team is mightily successful then all the peripherals will fall into place. I am a great lover of horse racing. In that sport I have heard so many people arguing over the name which should be given to a horse. I always tell them: 'It doesn't matter what it is called, as long as it becomes a champion. You can call it "Toast" if you want. As long as it wins regularly, nobody will complain.' For us, beating Australia had achieved that.

It was a long day. From Trafalgar Square we went to 10 Downing Street to meet the Prime Minister, and then on to Lord's where there was the symbolic gesture of handing back the Ashes to the MCC. I thought that I was tired but I can only imagine how those who had not slept the previous night felt. They must have slept well that night.

Marina and I were due to fly home to Cape Town on that Tuesday night. I had not even changed those travel plans when I had first heard of the bus parade being mooted. 'Wait until we win,' was my take. I did not want to be distracted from that.

That is also why I did not comment on the saga about my British passport in the lead-up to the Test. The story had re-emerged in the *Sunday Telegraph* just beforehand but had then been taken up by all and sundry within the media. It actually got out of hand on the Tuesday before the Test when reporters in South Africa began pestering my daughter, Nicola, who was looking after my house in Cape Town. I think that they thought that Marina was there and they wanted to question her about my family life. That was unacceptably intrusive in my opinion and I discovered who the reporter was and spoke to him personally.

During the celebrations on the Tuesday I received the good news, via a text message, that I am to receive a British passport. As if I was not having a good enough day anyway, then that made it even better. It has been a long story. All my grandparents were British. My late father, Desmond, had a British passport. My mother, Mary, who now lives in Durban, has a British passport. My two younger brothers, Gordon and Allan, and sister Ann all have British passports. Me? Not until now. Nor two other older brothers, John and Colin. You are probably wondering how some members of the family can have a British passport while others cannot. It has exercised some thinking in my mind over the years too. The reason why some siblings could receive British passports, and others could not, is given as depending when the individual was born. My two older brothers and I were born before 1 January 1949; we do not qualify. My two younger brothers and sister were born after that date; they do qualify. Confused? So I have always been. It is all to do with the Independence of India apparently. Goodness knows why.

And I was not alone in my incredulity. Indeed, I remember once being on tour in Pakistan with England and speaking to a member of the British High Commission about it. He was adamant that I could get a British passport. He checked it out and came back to me. 'You're right,' he said, 'you don't qualify.'

Of late the stumbling block has centred on how many days per year I actually spend in Britain. I first applied in 1991 but I really started to panic three years ago when I knew that my

Zimbabwean passport was about to expire. With the problems in that country I knew that it was highly unlikely that that would be renewed. I was right. It was not. Fortunately at that time I was able to obtain a South African passport.

To become a naturalised British citizen you must have lived in Britain for five years without spending more than 450 days out of the country within that period. That was obviously a problem for me. But most of the time I was spending outside of Britain was when I was away with the England cricket team. Yes, you can argue that I spend some time in my home in Cape Town, but it is very little, I can assure you. I am hardly ever there. My British summers are spent in Cardiff, where both Marina and I enjoy living. Although saying that, we spend more time in hotels scattered around the country than there in Wales, where we have a number of good friends. It is quiet and we can relax without too much disturbance. Now that I have been told that I will receive my British citizenship I may well buy a flat there.

But for now I do not have a permanent base here, so that is why I was keen to jet off quickly to Cape Town after the Ashes. That Tuesday night flight was not quite possible. I was required to conduct a short press conference on the Wednesday and then it was off on a British Airways flight that evening. First class, as well. That was a new experience. The England team always fly business class these days, but it was nice to be granted a step up. Anybody would think that something momentous had occurred.

But I realised that already. Things have definitely changed. I suppose that they did gradually throughout the summer. Just little things like walking across the train station at Paddington and having people shout out their congratulations and good luck. There was one text message which made me think, too. I am still very friendly with Mike Fatkin, the Glamorgan chief executive, from my time at the county and he texts me on a regular basis. But mainly they are mock-abusive texts, involving words like 'miserable git'. What, me? I usually chuckle to myself and don't bother to reply. There is usually very little I can say in reply. But after the win in the Trent Bridge Test, he sent me a very different text. It was much more serious, much more heartfelt. He sent his sincere congratulations, saying how proud he was. I am not saying that Fatkin cannot be serious or heartfelt, but our relationship has rarely run along those lines. Maybe I am reading too much into that one text, but it really made me sit up and think: 'This is becoming massive. We're on to something here.'

Talking of texts, they kept coming to Phil Neale from 'The Iceman'. Alan Chambers was with us all the way through, if only from a distance. At every turn he recognised a situation from his journey and related it to that which we were encountering. That was great to know, and provided excellent motivation, as well as a frequently good talking point.

People certainly wanted to talk to me after we had won the Ashes. Now people physically came up to me to say well done. That rarely happened before. I might have been recognised now and again, and heard people whispering: 'That's Duncan Fletcher, the England coach.' But now they were shaking my hand. It was a rather new experience. It happened at Heathrow as we waited for the plane. It happened again when we arrived in Cape Town.

I have never coveted fame and recognition. My personality dictates otherwise. And remember that I am only the coach. But, as long as it is rendered in a polite and sincere manner, then it would take a strange sort of character not to feel some satisfaction from it. But you always feel most satisfaction from the reaction of those closest to you. And the response of my family was incredible. They were there with me suffering the twists and turns of the summer.

My sister, Ann, took a day off work in Durban so that she could watch the whole of the final day's play on television. I don't think that my mother, Mary, missed a ball in her retirement home in Durban. She made sure that everyone there was supporting England. 'They're going crazy here,' she told me on the phone. All the others were watching too. Colin and his family in Switzerland; John, Gordon and Allan and their families in South Africa.

I hadn't quite expected the reception that greeted me when I stepped into my home in Cape Town either. 'Congratulations' banners and lots of Union Jacks adorned the walls, and sitting in the kitchen was a balloon, a 'Mr Incredible' balloon, with the word 'coach' added to it. I haven't seen that film *The Incredibles* but they tell me that it is about a family of undercover superheroes. I certainly do not consider myself one of them, but it is a neat way of summing up how I feel about my family. They are my superheroes.

My daughter Nicola and her husband Jared had been responsible for all the bunting. They also made me a card which I particularly liked, with a picture of the previously elusive urn on the front and a couple of good pictures of me on the back; one of them with my hands on my head in a seemingly exasperated manner, accompanied with the words: 'Nobody said it would be easy. 18 years had proven this.' But below was a happier picture and the words: 'But he knew it could be done and history was made.'

Nicola had sent Marina a text message during that final day at The Oval, probably just after lunch when the game was still in the balance: 'Physically sick but still watching.' As I said, the tension seems to affect the families more than the players and management.

But they could rest easy now, as I could back in Cape Town. But not before I had attended a benefit match for Jacques Kallis at Newlands. That was on the Friday after the Oval Test. Rather soon after it, you might well aver. But I did not consider it so, because I was honoured to be asked to be a nominal manager for the day. For that is all I was. It was not as if I was conducting the warm-up or anything quite as strenuous as that. Kallis was a player with whom I spent a lot of time when he was a youngster. And not just when he progressed to the Western Province side. He also attended the same school, Wynberg Boys' High School, as my son Michael. I was delighted to be present at the first of two matches in which Kallis's invitational side played against a South African XI. There were plenty of congratulations from everybody at Newlands. The series had been viewed with much enthusiasm in South Africa and from what I could gather most of the natives seemed to be supporting England. What did I say about Australia always being the team to beat?

After that it was time for some R and R. I needed that. I like time to reflect after a series and there has been no bigger series on which to do that. And there are so many things on which to reflect. But I look back with enormous pride. I see eleven fine individuals who have represented England for the bulk of the series. That is no disrespect to Paul Collingwood, who came in for the final Test and whose value I have already lauded.

In Michael Vaughan England have a captain of whom they can be immensely proud. There is no doubt in my mind that he is currently the best skipper in the world. He thoroughly out-captained Ricky Ponting in this series. That much will have been fairly obvious to you from events on the field, but I can also tell you that his man-management skills off the field were magnificent.

That is why I feel that it is an absolute travesty that he was not chosen to lead the Rest of the World team against Australia in the Super Series. Even if he was not going to lead, then he should have been in the squad for his batting alone. The selectors said that they were going to select players on the strength of their form against Australia. Well, is it my imagination or has Vaughan not done rather well against Australia in the two Test series in which he has played against them? He was not as prolific in 2005 as he had been in 2002/03 in Australia, but after two low scores at Lord's I thought that he played very well. You have got to remember that any captaincy burden is large, but in an Ashes series such as this it is onerous to the extreme. Vaughan showed his quality throughout the summer.

But still the 2005 series will probably be remembered as

'Freddie's Ashes' and I cannot disagree with that judgement. He was a colossus throughout. He might have been struggling a little with the bat at the start of the series but his two half-centuries at Edgbaston changed that, and changed the Australians' opinion of his batting too. From then on they realised that they were dealing with a supreme cricketer. His bowling just went from strength to strength. If I am truthful I would have preferred it that he did not appear in the Super Series. He would have been better off having a rest, otherwise with the Pakistan tour following hard on its heels he will have played almost continuous cricket from April until December.

Likewise with Steve Harmison: give him a rest. That would have been my preferred option for him in October. The reason again? That old chestnut of mine – mental tiredness.

Harmison started the series superbly at Lord's but thereafter probably did not capture as many wickets as he would have liked. However, he still retains that amazing ability to take crucial wickets at crucial times; remember that slower ball to deceive Michael Clarke at Edgbaston? With his pace and bounce he is always a threat. Sometimes with bowlers of that hostility, the others in the attack can feed off him. Maybe there are even times when the batsmen look to take extra liberties off other bowlers.

There were a number of England players who surprised the Australians. Both opening batsmen, Marcus Trescothick and Andrew Strauss, fall into that category. All those blithe comments beforehand from the Australian camp only served to inspire those two even more. They are a hugely dedicated pair of professionals, both full of determination and very strong mentally.

Simon Jones will probably fit into the same category. He surprised a lot of people on both sides. He is a world-class bowler now. End of story.

But for his namesake Geraint, the end of the tale is probably some way off. He knows that he needs to continue to work on his wicketkeeping, but there should be no doubt now that he is a quality batsman at this level. That partnership at Trent Bridge with Flintoff was crucial. Never forget that. Of all the twenty-two players out there performing in any one of the Tests, I think that he was the one under the most pressure. For him to produce the performances that he did, under that baleful scrutiny, only serves to underline further the strength of his character.

Ashley Giles also showed a similar sort of grit. He is always a useful member of the team, and don't forget that he took some very good catches too. He showed what it all meant to him when he caught Brett Lee at deep mid-wicket off Matthew Hoggard in the Oval Test. That celebration brought out much burning emotion from within; his later batting a continuation of that. For Hoggard that was not a conventional dismissal, but he had 'come to the party' (I haven't used that phrase enough in this book) at the right time. He had basically sat around for three Tests waiting for his opportunity before Trent Bridge. But then he grabbed it and finished strongly at The Oval.

Sadly that is not a comment I can make about Ian Bell, because he finished with a pair and there is no way of dressing that up. But as I have said, he is a young man with the skill and ability to come back from that. Playing your first full series against the Australians cannot have been easy.

Reading that last sentence has just made me realise that I have only mentioned ten players. Because there was someone who did find their maiden series a tad less arduous than Bell; that was Kevin Pietersen. I think that I have said enough about him already. He need not worry that I was going to omit him. He doesn't worry about anything at all actually.

But I do. I worry a little about the future. I worry that it is going to be difficult for cricketers and coaches to replicate the success of this series. Will there ever be another series like it? It is doubtful, certainly not in terms of excitement. There were three of the greatest Tests of all time in quick succession. Hyperbole? No. Remember that DVD I talked about at the end of chapter four? 'The Greatest Test'? They should have made two more entitled – 'A Greater Test' and then 'An Even Greater Test'. I see that they just settled for 'The Greatest Series'.

So the bar of expectation will be raised high. Everyone will be expected to score at over four runs an over in every Test. Anything less will be considered boring. You will hear shouts of 'Get on with it' if it is. But the run rate cannot always be so high. That is a fact. So please be patient. All you converts to the game, please realise that there will be some lulls. If you remember, there was the odd one in the summer of 2005.

Hang on. Was there though? Looking back I am not sure there was. Oh, what the heck. Full steam ahead.

It will be different, though, in Pakistan and India, where England travel next for two tricky tours against two very good teams. Different pitches, different challenges. Somebody has told me that I have nothing left to do now as England coach, that I have reached the summit. I have not. The one-day team has been making steady progress, but we still have work to do in that form of the game. The World Cup in 2007 must be an aim.

Somebody else also told me that England are still not officially ranked as the number one Test team in the world. Nothing left to do? That will have to be sorted. Sorry, Marina, we'll have to forget about that R and R. I've got some planning to do. Where are those videos of the Pakistan team?

# Statistical Appendix

England: Series averages

| Batting | M | Ins | NO | Runs | HS | Avge | 100 | 50 | Ct/St |
|---|---|---|---|---|---|---|---|---|---|
| K. Pietersen | 5 | 10 | 1 | 473 | 158 | 52.55 | 1 | 3 | 0 |
| M. Trescothick | 5 | 10 | 0 | 431 | 90 | 43.10 | 0 | 3 | 3 |
| A. Flintoff | 5 | 10 | 0 | 402 | 102 | 40.20 | 1 | 3 | 3 |
| A. Strauss | 5 | 10 | 0 | 393 | 129 | 39.30 | 2 | 0 | 6 |
| S. Jones | 4 | 6 | 4 | 66 | 20* | 33.00 | 0 | 0 | 1 |
| M. Vaughan | 5 | 10 | 0 | 326 | 166 | 32.60 | 1 | 1 | 2 |
| G. Jones | 5 | 10 | 1 | 229 | 85 | 25.44 | 0 | 1 | 15/1 |
| A. Giles | 5 | 10 | 2 | 155 | 59 | 19.37 | 0 | 1 | 5 |
| I. Bell | 5 | 10 | 0 | 171 | 65 | 17.10 | 0 | 2 | 8 |
| S. Harmison | 5 | 8 | 2 | 60 | 20* | 10.00 | 0 | 0 | 1 |
| P. Collingwood | 1 | 2 | 0 | 17 | 10 | 8.50 | 0 | 0 | 1 |
| M. Hoggard | 5 | 9 | 2 | 45 | 16 | 6.42 | 0 | 0 | 0 |

| Bowling | M | Ovs | Mds | Runs | Wkts | Best | Avge | 5i | 10m |
|---|---|---|---|---|---|---|---|---|---|
| S. Jones | 4 | 102 | 17 | 378 | 18 | 6–53 | 21.00 | 2 | 0 |
| A. Flintoff | 5 | 194 | 32 | 655 | 24 | 5–78 | 27.29 | 1 | 0 |
| M. Hoggard | 5 | 122.1 | 15 | 473 | 16 | 4–97 | 29.56 | 0 | 0 |
| S. Harmison | 5 | 161.1 | 22 | 549 | 17 | 5–43 | 32.29 | 1 | 0 |
| A. Giles | 5 | 160 | 18 | 578 | 10 | 3–78 | 57.80 | 0 | 0 |
| P. Collingwood | 1 | 4 | 0 | 17 | 0 | — | — | 0 | 0 |
| I. Bell | 5 | 7 | 2 | 20 | 0 | — | — | 0 | 0 |
| M. Vaughan | 5 | 5 | 0 | 21 | 0 | — | — | 0 | 0 |

* = not out

## Australia: Series averages

| Batting | M | Ins | NO | Runs | HS | Avge | 100 | 50 | Ct/St |
|---|---|---|---|---|---|---|---|---|---|
| J. Langer | 5 | 10 | 1 | 394 | 105 | 43.77 | 1 | 2 | 2 |
| R. Ponting | 5 | 9 | 0 | 359 | 156 | 39.88 | 1 | 1 | 4 |
| M. Clarke | 5 | 9 | 0 | 335 | 91 | 37.22 | 0 | 2 | 2 |
| G. McGrath | 3 | 5 | 4 | 36 | 20* | 36.00 | 0 | 0 | 1 |
| M. Hayden | 5 | 10 | 1 | 318 | 138 | 35.33 | 1 | 0 | 10 |
| S. Warne | 5 | 9 | 0 | 249 | 90 | 27.66 | 0 | 1 | 5 |
| S. Katich | 5 | 9 | 0 | 248 | 67 | 27.55 | 0 | 2 | 4 |
| B. Lee | 5 | 9 | 3 | 158 | 47 | 26.33 | 0 | 0 | 2 |
| A. Gilchrist | 5 | 9 | 1 | 181 | 49* | 22.62 | 0 | 0 | 18/1 |
| D. Martyn | 5 | 9 | 0 | 178 | 65 | 19.77 | 0 | 1 | 4 |
| M. Kasprowicz | 2 | 4 | 0 | 44 | 20 | 11.00 | 0 | 0 | 3 |
| S. Tait | 2 | 3 | 2 | 8 | 4 | 8.00 | 0 | 0 | 0 |
| J. Gillespie | 3 | 6 | 0 | 47 | 26 | 7.83 | 0 | 0 | 1 |

| Bowling | M | Ovs | Mds | Runs | Wkts | Best | Avge | 5i | 10m |
|---|---|---|---|---|---|---|---|---|---|
| R. Ponting | 5 | 6 | 2 | 9 | 1 | 1–9 | 9.00 | 0 | 0 |
| S. Warne | 5 | 252.5 | 37 | 797 | 40 | 6–46 | 19.92 | 3 | 2 |
| G. McGrath | 3 | 134 | 22 | 440 | 19 | 5–53 | 23.15 | 2 | 0 |
| B. Lee | 5 | 191.1 | 25 | 822 | 20 | 4–82 | 41.10 | 0 | 0 |
| S. Tait | 2 | 48 | 5 | 210 | 5 | 3–97 | 42.00 | 0 | 0 |
| S. Katich | 5 | 12 | 1 | 50 | 1 | 1–36 | 50.00 | 0 | 0 |
| M. Kasprowicz | 2 | 52 | 6 | 250 | 4 | 3–80 | 62.50 | 0 | 0 |
| J. Gillespie | 3 | 67 | 6 | 300 | 3 | 2–91 | 100.00 | 0 | 0 |
| M. Clarke | 5 | 2 | 0 | 6 | 0 | — | — | 0 | 0 |

* = not out

## Highest individual scores

*Qualification: 50 runs*

| | | | | |
|---|---|---|---|---|
| 166 | M. Vaughan | ENG | Old Trafford | Third Test, 1st innings |
| 158 | K. Pietersen | ENG | The Oval | Fifth Test, 2nd innings |
| 156 | R. Ponting | AUS | Old Trafford | Third Test, 2nd innings |
| 138 | M. Hayden | AUS | The Oval | Fifth Test, 1st innings |
| 129 | A. Strauss | ENG | The Oval | Fifth Test, 1st innings |
| 106 | A. Strauss | ENG | Old Trafford | Third Test, 2nd innings |
| 105 | J. Langer | AUS | The Oval | Fifth Test, 1st innings |
| 102 | A. Flintoff | ENG | Trent Bridge | Fourth Test, 1st innings |
| 91 | M. Clarke | AUS | Lord's | First Test, 2nd innings |
| 90 | M. Trescothick | ENG | Edgbaston | Second Test, 1st innings |
| 90 | S. Warne | AUS | Old Trafford | Third Test, 1st innings |
| 85 | G. Jones | ENG | Trent Bridge | Fourth Test, 1st innings |
| 82 | J. Langer | AUS | Edgbaston | Second Test, 1st innings |
| 73 | A. Flintoff | ENG | Edgbaston | Second Test, 2nd innings |
| 72 | A. Flintoff | ENG | The Oval | Fifth Test, 1st innings |
| 71 | K. Pietersen | ENG | Edgbaston | Second Test, 1st innings |
| 68 | A. Flintoff | ENG | Edgbaston | Second Test, 1st innings |
| 67 | S. Katich | AUS | Lord's | First Test, 2nd innings |
| 65 | D. Martyn | AUS | Lord's | First Test, 2nd innings |
| 65 | I. Bell | ENG | Old Trafford | Third Test, 2nd innings |
| 65 | M. Trescothick | ENG | Trent Bridge | Fourth Test, 1st innings |
| 64* | K. Pietersen | ENG | Lord's | First Test, 2nd innings |
| 63 | M. Trescothick | ENG | Old Trafford | Third Test, 1st innings |
| 61 | R. Ponting | AUS | Edgbaston | Second Test, 1st innings |
| 61 | J. Langer | AUS | Trent Bridge | Fourth Test, 2nd innings |
| 59 | I. Bell | ENG | Old Trafford | Third Test, 1st innings |
| 59 | S. Katich | AUS | Trent Bridge | Fourth Test, 2nd innings |
| 59 | A. Giles | ENG | The Oval | Fifth Test, 2nd innings |
| 58 | M. Vaughan | ENG | Trent Bridge | Fourth Test, 1st innings |
| 57 | K. Pietersen | ENG | Lord's | First Test, 1st innings |
| 56 | M. Clarke | AUS | Trent Bridge | Fourth Test, 2nd innings |

## Best bowling figures

*Qualification: 4 wickets in an innings*

| 6–46 | S. Warne | AUS | Edgbaston | Second Test, 2nd innings |
| **6–53** | **S. Jones** | **ENG** | **Old Trafford** | **Third Test, 1st innings** |
| 6–122 | S. Warne | AUS | The Oval | Fifth Test, 1st innings |
| 6–124 | S. Warne | AUS | The Oval | Fifth Test, 2nd innings |
| **5–43** | **S. Harmison** | **ENG** | **Lord's** | **First Test, 1st innings** |
| **5–44** | **S. Jones** | **ENG** | **Trent Bridge** | **Fourth Test, 1st innings** |
| 5–53 | G. McGrath | AUS | Lord's | First Test, 1st innings |
| **5–78** | **A. Flintoff** | **ENG** | **The Oval** | **Fifth Test, 1st innings** |
| 5–115 | G. McGrath | AUS | Old Trafford | Third Test, 2nd innings |
| 4–29 | G. McGrath | AUS | Lord's | First Test, 2nd innings |
| 4–31 | S. Warne | AUS | Trent Bridge | Fourth Test, 2nd innings |
| 4–64 | S. Warne | AUS | Lord's | First Test, 2nd innings |
| **4–71** | **A. Flintoff** | **ENG** | **Old Trafford** | **Third Test, 2nd innings** |
| **4–79** | **A. Flintoff** | **ENG** | **Edgbaston** | **Second Test, 2nd innings** |
| 4–82 | B. Lee | AUS | Edgbaston | Second Test, 2nd innings |
| **4–97** | **M. Hoggard** | **ENG** | **The Oval** | **Fifth Test, 1st innings** |
| 4–99 | S. Warne | AUS | Old Trafford | Third Test, 1st innings |
| 4–100 | B. Lee | AUS | Old Trafford | Third Test, 1st innings |
| 4–102 | S. Warne | AUS | Trent Bridge | Fourth Test, 1st innings |
| 4–116 | S. Warne | AUS | Edgbaston | Second Test, 1st innings |

## Highest partnerships per wicket

### England

| | | | | |
|---|---|---|---|---|
| 1st | 112 | Trescothick & Strauss | Edgbaston | Second Test, 1st innings |
| 2nd | 137 | Trescothick & Vaughan | Old Trafford | Third Test, 1st innings |
| 3rd | 127 | Vaughan & Bell | Old Trafford | Third Test, 1st innings |
| | 127 | Strauss & Bell | Old Trafford | Third Test, 2nd innings |
| 4th | 67 | Vaughan & Pietersen | Trent Bridge | Fourth Test, 1st innings |
| 5th | 143 | Strauss & Flintoff | The Oval | Fifth Test, 1st innings |
| 6th | 177 | Flintoff & G. Jones | Trent Bridge | Fourth Test, 1st innings |
| 7th | 87 | Flintoff & G. Jones | Old Trafford | Third Test, 1st innings |
| 8th | 109 | Pietersen & Giles | The Oval | Fifth Test, 2nd innings |
| 9th | 27 | Hoggard & Harmison | Edgbaston | Second Test, 1st innings |
| | 27 | Giles & Hoggard | The Oval | Fifth Test, 2nd innings |
| 10th | 51 | Flintoff & S. Jones | Edgbaston | Second Test, 2nd innings |

### Australia

| | | | | |
|---|---|---|---|---|
| 1st | 185 | Langer & Hayden | The Oval | Fifth Test, 1st innings |
| 2nd | 88 | Langer & Ponting | Edgbaston | Second Test, 1st innings |
| 3rd | 46 | Ponting & Martyn | Lord's | First Test, 2nd innings |
| 4th | 155 | Martyn & Clarke | Lord's | First Test, 2nd innings |
| 5th | 100 | Clarke & Katich | Trent Bridge | Fourth Test, 2nd innings |
| 6th | 81 | Ponting & Clarke | Old Trafford | Third Test, 2nd innings |
| 7th | 49 | Katich & Warne | Lord's | First Test, 1st innings |
| 8th | 86 | Warne & Gillespie | Old Trafford | Third Test, 1st innings |
| 9th | 52 | Gillespie & McGrath | Lord's | First Test, 2nd innings |
| 10th | 59 | Lee & Kasprowicz | Edgbaston | Second Test, 2nd innings |

# Picture Credits

1: Tom Shaw/AP/Empics; 2, 3: Alastair Grant/AP/Empics; 4, 20, 43, 44, 45: Matt Dunham/AP/Empics; 5, 13, 14, 15, 16, 24: Neal Simpson/Empics; 6, 22, 25: Nick Potts/PA/Empics; 7, 10, 47: Chris Young/PA/Empics; 8, 9: Sean Dempsey/PA/Empics; 11, 12, 17, 18, 19, 36, 46: Rui Vieira/PA/Empics; 21, 26, 28, 29: Phil Noble/PA/Empics; 23, 27, 30, 31, 33, 34, 35, 39: Jon Super/AP/Empics; 32: David Davies/PA/Empics; 37, 40, 41: Jon Buckle/Empics; 38, 42: Max Nash/AP/Empics; 42: Clive Rose/Getty Images; 48, 49: Tom Shaw/Getty Images/PA/Pool; 50: Action Images/Oliver Greenwood.